DEM●S

Demos is an independent think tank committed to radical thinking on the long-term problems facing the UK and other advanced industrial societies.

It aims to develop ideas – both theoretical and practical – to help shape the politics of the twenty first century, and to improve the breadth and quality of political debate.

Demos publishes books and a regular journal and undertakes substantial empirical and policy oriented research projects. Demos is a registered charity.

In all its work Demos brings together people from a wide range of backgrounds in business, academia, government, the voluntary sector and the media to share and cross-fertilise ideas and experiences.

For further information and
subscription details please contact:
Demos
Panton House
25 Haymarket
London SW1Y 4EN
Telephone: 0171 321 2200
Facsimile: 0171 321 2342
email: mail@demos.co.uk

Other publications available from Demos:

Civic Entrepreneurship
The Employee Mutual
A Piece of the Action
The Rise of the Social Entrepreneur

To order a publication or
a free catalogue please contact
Demos (details overleaf).

To our mutual advantage

Charles Leadbeater and Ian Christie

First published in 1999 by
Demos
Panton House
25 Haymarket
London SW1Y 4EN
Telephone: 0171 321 2200
Facsimile: 0171 321 2342
email: mail@demos.co.uk

ISBN 1 898309 84 1
Printed in Great Britain by Redwood Books
Design by Lindsay Nash

Contents

Acknowledgements

This report was made possible by generous grants from the Calouste Gulbenkian Foundation, the Building Societies Trust, the Nationwide Building Society and the NatWest Group.

Lisa Barclay played an invaluable role in researching much of the basic data on mutuals contained in the report. We are very grateful to the many people who gave their time as interviewees and who provided us with documentary material.

Thanks also to staff at Demos who helped to produce this report, particularly Lindsay Nash, Geoff Mulgan and Tom Bentley.

1. The state of mutuality

Introduction

Mutual organisations, organised for and often by their members, are regularly pronounced to be dead or dying. Several leading building societies have become shareholder-owned banks and some leading mutual insurers have de-mutualised. Co-operative retailers have a smaller share of the market than twenty years ago and trade union membership has declined markedly. The friendly societies, which were the backbone of insurance and welfare provision in the last century, are a shadow of their former selves. The reverses suffered by older mutuals are often used as evidence that *all* mutuals are in decline, across the economy.

This report shows that these obituaries are premature. We present the first comprehensive survey of the state of health of mutual organisations, which shows mutuals play a critical role in providing many of the most fundamental services we rely upon. Mutuals help provide childcare and adult education. They help to organise community safety and local economic development. People turn to mutuals for health insurance, life assurance and mortgages. Some of the most promising approaches to primary health and social housing are offered by co-operatives and mutuals. And in the business sector, electronic mutuals organised over the Internet and employee owned businesses are among the most dynamic organisations in the fastest growing sectors of the economy.

Mutual organisations take many forms, from co-operatives to trade unions, building societies and employee owned businesses. A mutual is organised to serve its members, whether they are consumers (as in mutual insurance), employees (as in worker owned companies) or suppliers (for example in some agricultural co-operatives). Mutuals are organised for and often by their members, who band together with the common purpose of providing a shared service from which they all benefit. Their main competitors are traditional companies, which are run by managers who are ultimately accountable to shareholders, and public sector organisations, which are run by civil servants, overseen by politicians and financed by taxpayers. Our research shows the spirit of mutual aid and co-operative enterprise is alive and well in the UK across a diverse range of communities and markets. Mutuals – when they are well run, when they serve the appropriate markets and when they are organised on the right scale – have significant advantages over the private and public sector organisations with which they compete. This report argues that mutuals can do more than survive; they can thrive in the twenty-first century service economy, because at their best they can harness two ingredients critical to success for modern enterprise – *trust* and *know-how.*

We estimate that membership of the mutual sector – organisations that are owned by their members or that are run with a mutual ethos – stands at more than 30 million; mutual organisations have a turnover of at least £25 billion and employ at least 250,000 people across a broad range of fields.

There were 544 co-operatives or jointly controlled farm businesses in 1997, with a turnover of £7.4 billion and 243,000 members. Co-operatives had a monopoly in marketing wool; the Milk Marque, a co-operative with 18,000 farmer members handles 7 billion litres of milk; farm co-operatives accounted for 95 per cent of apples, 74 per cent of cauliflowers, 63 per cent of raspberries, 60 per cent of lettuces, 57 per cent of peas and 50 per cent of pears. At the end of 1997 co-operative retailers had 6 per cent of the grocery market, a larger share than Morrisons, Waitrose, Iceland or Marks & Spencer. Retail co-operatives employ about 120,000 people, with revenues of about £8.5 billion and account for 4 per cent of British retailing. This is just an illustration of the range of activities organised by mutuals.

In February 1998 there were 694,423 children in 18,000 community based pre-school learning groups in which parents help to finance and run. The Kids Club Network estimates that 637 clubs for school-age children, with 14,788 children taking part, are run by parents as mutuals. The Workers' Educational Association, one of the largest adult education providers, has 116,000 students a year in 650 branches, run mainly run by volunteer members working in tandem with full-time support staff. The University of the Third Age, which relies on high-levels of member input to fund-raising and management, offers about 150 courses, through 365 branches with 65,000 members.

The 139 development trusts, with assets of £160 million and an annual income of about £30 million, employ about 1,840 people and have 18,600 members. Development trusts, which are non-profit making and accountable to a community membership, acquire income-generating assets on the community's behalf. By the end of 1999 there should be 54 community foundations in the UK, covering 60 per cent of the UK population, using donations from local people to fund a range community developments. In 1997–98 they had an income of £30 million and made grants of £12.4 million. The largest, the Tyne and Wear Foundation, has an endowment of £18 million and made 500 grants with a combined value of more than £1 million in 1997–98. There are five community loan funds in the UK and at least 65 settlement and social action centres with assets of about £13.4 million and income of about £17.6 million.

The 70 remaining building societies had 2.8 million borrowers, 19 million investors and 37,309 employees at the end of 1997 and accounted for 17 per cent of retail deposits (£98.6 billion) and 23 per cent of outstanding residential mortgages (£105.34 billion). Some of the largest insurance companies are mutuals designed to benefit policy-holders. Standard Life, for example, the largest mutual life assurance company, has assets of £50 billion, and £60 billion under management for 4 million customers. The mutual insurers which include Equitable Life, Friends Provident, Scottish Life, Scottish Widows and the Royal London, account for at least a quarter of the market. The Co-operative Insurance Society, which is wholly owned by the Co-operative Wholesale Society, has 3 million customers, an annual turnover of about £2 billion and manages investments for customers worth about £17 billion.

The 80 largest friendly societies have £11.43 billion under management, 11.1 million policies, 4.76 million members and an income of

£2.849 billion. They pay annual benefits worth £867.6 million. There are 584 credit unions with 214,660 members and deposits of £105.8 million. About 30 per cent of employees (7 million people) are members of a trade union.

Crime prevention schemes increasingly include mutual community security. About 120,000 Neighbourhood Watch schemes cover 5 million homes, about 25 per cent of the population. About 20,000 also have a 'street watch' which includes, for example, escort services for older people. Mutuality is central to primary and public health services. About 300 community well-being centres and co-operatives provide basic health and social care in England and Wales. About 4,500 of the 20,000 general practitioners in England and Wales are in co-operatives to improve out-of-surgery-hours visiting services. In 1996–97 about 6 million people (10 per cent of the population) were members of mutual cash benefit schemes to cover periods of illness. Co-operatives play a significant role in social housing provision and tenants' management organisations have been shown to be far more effective providers of social housing than local authorities.

Mutual organisations are in far better health, across a much wider range of sectors, than most people think. The extent and role of mutuals are set out in the accompanying table (see Figure 1).

Mutuality, ideology and organisation

The idea of mutuality has many attractions because it seems to combine the promise of social cohesion and self-organisation within a market economy. That is why mutuality could provide the heart to the idea of the 'third way' or radical-centre proposed by Tony Blair and Gerhard Schroeder. Mutuals are often outside and at odds with the bureaucracy of the public sector, because they stress the value of voluntary, collaborative action. Mutuals provide social provision and collective services but are outside the state. Yet the mutual ethos also rejects the individualism and consumerism of the market. They are an alternative to both the paternalism of public services and the privatism of the market because mutuals stress the value of co-operative, often local, solutions to shared problems.

As Ian Hargreaves points out in his account on the role of co-operatives in tackling social exclusion:

The co-operative movement was based upon the instinct that in your own town, your own community, the solution to immediate problems of work, finance, housing, family instability and self-respect lay within your own grasp; that the only solutions to trust are those you design yourself and for which you take responsibility. This is the co-operative spirit: men and women taking charge of a situation, answerable to each other, working through democratic structures of accountability. [1]

The traditional case for mutuality has been reinforced from a variety of sources. Amitai Etzioni and Geoff Mulgan argue that mutual responsibility is the ethical foundation of a strong, democratic community (as opposed to, for example, rights or consumer choice) and that mutuality can promote a cumulative growth in trust which enables a community to tackle its shared problems more effectively.[2] Economists and business theorists, such as John Kay and Thomas Kochan, argue that successful companies and economies foster collaboration by offering mutual gains to their different stakeholders.[3] The case for mutuality has been made by evolutionary biologists,[4] social psychologists[5] and game theorists[6] who argue that co-operative, win-win solutions to problems are often more efficient than competition which generates winners and losers. Anthony Giddens takes a similar tack, arguing that market societies need to balance a culture of individualism with 'civic liberalism' to build a healthier sense of community.[7]

There is little doubting the ideological and ethical appeal of mutuality. Yet it is far harder to show that mutual organisations are effective in practice. This report does not aim to add to the theoretical debate about mutuality. Instead it examines the strengths and weaknesses of mutual organisations across a wide range of services. Our focus is the organisational capacity of mutuals to solve problems more effectively than their main competitors: the traditional public sector or investor-owned companies. That organisational capacity will determine whether they could play a larger role, as advocates of mutuality maintain.

Mutual organisations, whatever their core purpose, operate in a competitive environment. They have distinct strengths and weaknesses, which stem from the way they involve their members. If mutuals develop these strengths, minimise their weaknesses and choose their markets wisely, they will prosper. If mutuals neglect these

Figure 1. Mutuals in Britain 1999 (1)

	Mutual Orgs	Market Share	Turnover Annual	Membership	Employees
Agriculture	544 (2)	95% apples 85% milk 74% cauliflowers	£7.4bn	243,000	13,300
Retailing	46 4,600 outlets	6% grocery 4% retail as a whole	£5.2bn £8.5bn	9m	120,000
Employee owned businesses					
Worker co-ops	1,500				15,000
ESOPs	100 (3)				
LETS	270			1.2m	19,450
Housing					
Social housing (Co-operatives and Housing association)		5%		1m dwellings 120,000 cooperatives	
Tenant management organisations	150				
Self-build	60 (4)				
Health					
Cash benefit schemes		10% of adult pop		6m	
Community well-being and health centres	300				
Self-help groups	2–3,000				
Contact a Family	1,300				
Education/childcare					
Pre-school groups	18,000	19% of Under-fives		694,423 children 1m parents	
Mutual kids' clubs	637			14,788	

	Mutual Orgs	Market Share	Turnover Annual	Membership	Employees
Adult education					
Workers Education Association	650 branches		£13m +	116,000 students p.a.	
University of the Third Age	365			65,000	
Crime					
Neighbourhood Watch (Incl Street Watch)	120,000 20,000	25%		5m homes	
Mediation schemes	150				
Crime prevention partnerships	250				**Assets**
Employment					
Trade unions	233	30%	£684m	7m	£88m
Community development					
Development trusts	139		£30m	18,600	£160m
Community trusts and Foundations	54 (5)	60% of adult pop	£30m	£65m	
Community loan funds	5				£75m
Financial services					
Friendly societies	293		£2.8bn	4.8m	£12bn
Building societies	70	23%		2.8m borrowers 19 savers	
Mutual insurers	25+	27%			
Credit unions	584		£105.8m	214,660	

1. These figures are derived from a variety of sources many o which do not provide full or easily reconciled figures. All the figures in the table are quoted in the full text of the report, with references.
2. 1997 Figures from the Plunkett Foundation Annual Report.
3. The number of Esops is much larger, probably 670, but most of these are financial vehciles to distribute shares to employees.
4. The number of community self-build schemes under way each year.
5. End of 1999.

distinctive strengths, deploy them in the wrong markets or over-stretch themselves, mutuals may be over-taken by the competition. It is widely thought that mutuals have been pushed to the margins by the private and public sectors. Investor-owned companies seem to be more focused, efficient, customer-driven, innovative and richer. In welfare, the state has expanded its activities this century at the expense of charities and voluntary self-help. Our research shows that mutuals, large and small, have more strength, dynamism and potential than the conventional wisdom allows for.

There is no denying that mutual, member-owned organisations often suffer from distinctive weaknesses: they are prone to become inward looking and conservative, serving their existing, 'insider' members rather than innovating to recruit new members. Small mutuals, with a powerful sense of membership can lack sufficient scale to make the most of their skills and ethos; large mutuals often have a highly diluted sense of membership.

Yet mutuals also have significant, distinctive strengths, which equip them well for modern tasks. The best mutuals can call upon the know-how and ideas of their members. They use their membership structure to unlock innovation. As mutuals are not in business to serve share-holders they can command people's trust and commitment in a way that traditional companies find hard. People often join a mutual because they share a sense of identity and purpose with its other members; private and public organisations often lack this 'relational' quality.

Mutuals such as credit unions can reach economically marginalised parts of society in ways that the public and private sectors cannot match; they can make up for the myriad failures of private business and public services to provide what many citizens and communities need and can afford. Mutuals can and will be pioneers in opening up new areas of the 'social economy' – as in the development of crime preven-tion initiatives and new environmental services. The spirit of mutual-ity is ideally suited to electronic commerce and the Internet: one of the largest and most successful mutuals in the world is the club that produced the Linux software, now running on more than 10 million computers worldwide. As we show, there are opportunities for mutuals to organise groups of consumers in liberalised utility markets, as well as to deliver a wide range of services previously provided by the state.

2. When mutuals work (and fail)

Advocates of mutuality are sometimes their own worst enemies. When they oversell the advantages of mutuality, by presenting it as an elixir that naturally combines ethics with efficiency, they risk claiming too much. Mutuals, as with other organisations such as investor-owned companies, have weaknesses as well as strengths. The performance of mutuals depends on how they use their strengths and minimise their weaknesses. To assess the role that mutuals could play in Britain we must answer five related questions:

- What is a mutual?
- What is distinctive about mutuals?
- What special strengths do mutuals have?
- In which markets, providing which services, will this competitive advantage be played out to greatest advantage?
- What distinctive weaknesses do mutuals suffer from?

Mutuality defined

Mutual organisations come in many shapes and sizes, exhibiting degrees of mutuality. Some are mutually owned by their members. Others exhibit a mutual ethos although they may not be owned by members. Let's start with ownership.

A mutual organisation is owned by its members, who also have a say – usually a vote – in the corporate governance of the organisation, for example, by voting in elections for a board of directors. But this does not define a mutual: many shareholder owned companies would fit that description. (Shareholders are strictly speaking members of the company they own and have a vote at annual general meetings.) The distinguishing feature of a mutual is that the member-owners are more than investors. They usually have another relationship with the mutual either as consumers, producers or suppliers. The members create and own the organisation either to consume its services or to come together as joint-producers. A consumer-mutual, for example, is owned by members who are also consumers of the services the organisation provides. Mutually owned building societies and insurance companies fit into this category: their savers or policy-holders own them. A producer-mutual, for example, is owned by its members who are also its employees or suppliers. An employee-owned company fits this description, as do many farm co-operatives, which pool and market the output of their member farms.

In practice, however, ownership is just one, albeit critical, aspect of mutuality. Many organisations adhere to mutual principles in the way they are run, without being mutually owned. Charities, trusts and clubs, for example, which have no owners can adhere to mutual principles by allowing volunteers or members a vote in elections for office holders and by involving volunteers in production. The Workers' Educational Association follows mutual principles because many of its courses are organised by volunteers who are former students. A public sector organisation can have a mutual ethos even if it is owned by the state. A school, for example, can involve its parents in decision-making through the Parent Teacher Association, parental votes for the board of governors and by engaging parents in fund-raising, auxiliary teaching and extra-curricular activities. A school that was rich in parental involvement would not count as a mutual – in formal terms – but it would be run in a mutual spirit and would depend, to some extent, on a mutual organisation like the Parent–Teacher Association. Even commercial businesses, owned by investors, can make profits by dealing with staff, suppliers, partners and community groups in a mutual manner to deliver mutual gains. This mutual approach to managing relationships between companies and suppliers, partners and employees is increasingly important.

Mutuality comes in degrees. The narrowest definition of a mutual – a strong mutual – is an organisation owned and governed by members who either are its consumers, producers, employees or suppliers. Other organisations, which are part of the public sector, public–private joint ventures, charities or even investor-owned companies, can embody a weaker form of mutuality if they are run with a mutual ethos. As we shall see, the strongest form of mutuality – based on ownership – is sometimes the narrowest and not necessarily the most potent. 'Weaker' or less formal models of mutuality – which promote a culture of co-operative self-help – may be more flexible and dynamic. The most dynamic mutuals combine a common ownership structure with a mutual culture and management style that promotes a sense of membership and collaboration among staff, suppliers, partners and consumers.

What is distinctive about mutuals?

Organisations bring together financiers and investors, managers and workers, consumers and suppliers. All organisations, public, private or mutual, are sets of relationships. Mutuals create a set of relationships between owners, workers and consumers that is quite different from the 'model' investor-owned company.

In the UK, a publicly quoted company is owned by outside investors, whose prime interest is to earn a financial return. The owners delegate their authority to a board of directors, who appoint managers to run the business. The key issues for the investor-owned business are how the owners monitor, reward and control managers. The advantages of investor-ownership, in principle, are that it creates focused, efficient, well-capitalised organisations that are kept on their toes by their demanding but detached owners. Of course life is not that simple. The real ownership of private sector companies is far less clear cut than this model implies. In practice the rights of shareholder owners are quite limited. Many investor-owned companies often fail to reap the advantages of this form of organisation.

Mutuals are different because they orchestrate relations between owners, staff and consumers in a quite different way. Mutuals are designed to serve their members, not potentially footloose investors. In the case of 'strong mutuals', the owner-members are usually consumers, employees or suppliers. They should have a regular and reasonably close relationship with the organisation. That should make it easier for them to monitor the performance of the managers than it is for outside investors. Mutuals should stand out by the way they involve their members, not just in the formal procedures of corporate governance but in the day-to-day running of a mutual. The immediate goal of a 'competitive mutual' is to provide a service that matches the quality of competing offerings provided by the public and private sector, whether that is in financial services, housing, health care or childcare. In these situations mutuals are distinguished by the way they operate. Often in a consumer mutual, for example, the members are co-producers of the service they consume. For example, pre-school play groups that are run and funded by parents have to compete with private and public nursery provision. What stands out about mutual approaches to childcare is the way that parental involvement changes the nature of the service. In 'community mutuals' such as community foundations or development trusts, what stands out about mutuals is their capacity to gather people around a common sense of purpose. It is not just the way in which they operate that matters, but how they are constituted.

Mutual strength
The membership base of a mutual should give it two advantages over traditional investor-owned companies and public sector organisations: access to deeper reservoirs of *trust* and *know-how* among its members.

First, a mutual should find it easier to win the trust of its members, especially when there is a risk they might be exploited by a private or public monopoly. Mutuals often emerge in response to so-called 'market failure'. This is one reason why consumer co-operatives are so common among farmers in the US. When commercial fertilisers and feedstuffs were introduced at the beginning of the twentieth century, US farmers found it difficult to check on their quality. As a consequence most fertilisers were of poor quality as the producers found it easy to exploit unknowing consumers. In response, farmers formed co-operatives to make and supply fertilisers so they could be confident of the quality of the fertilisers they bought. The farmers trusted a mutual, of which they were members; they could not trust an investor-owned company, which did not have their interests at heart. Something similar happened to the life insurance industry in the US.

Life insurance was first sold in the United States in 1810. Until 1843 a number of well-capitalised, conservatively managed, investor-owned companies tried to sell life insurance. Despite their conservative credentials none of these companies sold more than a few hundred policies in more than three decades. Potential policy-holders did not trust the companies not to run off with their money, because the companies were responsible, in the last resort, to their shareholders. That changed in 1843 when the first mutual life insurer was formed. By 1847 there were seven mutuals owned by their policy-holders and by 1849 there were nineteen. The original seven mutuals are still in business. Most of the investor-owned companies had stopped selling life insurance by 1853. Eventually life insurance spread to millions of people, largely because consumers felt they could trust mutuals in a way that they could not, at the time, trust an investor-owned company. As with building societies, friendly societies and co-operative retailing in the UK, the organisational innovation of a 'mutual' created an entire industry.[8]

As long as there are threats of private or public monopolies, there will be scope for mutuals. The co-operative development of Linux software was led by computer users frustrated by Microsoft's dominance. They did not want to make money but to create more functional, effective software. Credit unions have formed in poorer areas in British cities in response to market failure. Often poor people find it hard to get mainstream credit and are exploited by loan sharks. A mutual is an obvious response.

Public sector monopoly can be as threatening as private sector monopoly. Mutuals often emerge in health, education, welfare and housing in reaction to perceived failings on the part of the state. Patients with special needs, for example, often complain that public services are too inflexible to serve them properly, while private provision is too expensive. As a result patients with special needs feel neglected and under-served. One response is to form a self-help organisation with people with similar needs. Such mutuals are increasingly common in health care as a complement to state-run services. Mutuals, as we shall see, are often formed in response to 'state-failure' rather than 'market-failure'.

Second, mutuals should be better placed to tap into members' know-how and ideas. The member-ownership of a mutual should, in principle, help it tap greater loyalty and innovation than a traditional company. As a result mutuals should, in theory, be especially well-placed to create a virtuous spiral of trust, loyalty and innovation by involving their members. The prospect of mutual gain should be an incentive for the members to contribute to improving a mutual's performance through their ideas and know-how. By involving their members, mutuals should be able to unlock ideas among individuals and whole communities, which investor-owned companies and public sector bureaucracies cannot reach. This is a central component of the case for employee ownership, especially in knowledge-based businesses, where the know-how of employees is critical to the competitiveness of the business. But it is also central to the way community development initiatives work.

Where mutuals prosper

Mutuals are often dismissed as old-fashioned. Yet mutuals are not alone in having Victorian roots. Many of our other large organisations – universities, civil service departments, even investor-owned companies – also have their origins in the last century. Mutuals – such as Linux – are well suited to the competitive conditions of the modern economy, in which know-how, innovation and customer loyalty are critical to competitiveness. Mutuals could prosper in the knowledge-driven economy just as they did in the nineteenth century in quite different conditions.

Companies increasingly compete on their ability to develop, generate, deploy and exploit their distinctive know-how and competencies. These intangible assets are as important as traditional assets such as machinery, equipment, land and labour, which in an open market economy are usually available to a company's competitors on equal terms. Intangible assets, such as know-how, a brand reputation or customer-loyalty, are difficult for competitors to imitate. Mutuals that trade on their ability to win their members' trust and garner their ideas are competing on the basis of intangible assets, which are of greatest value in the modern economy.

Mutuals prosper not just in the context of state or market failure but where organisations need to garner the tacit knowledge and commitment of consumers or producers. Linux became the world's fastest growing computer operating system because of its ability to draw upon the know-how and expertise of thousands of volunteer member programmers. This capacity to draw upon the diverse, often tacit and informal skills of members is at the heart of the role mutuals could play in tackling social and financial exclusion. deep-seated social problems are often complex and compounded – poor education and housing leading to joblessness, poverty and ill-health. Tackling such Deep-seated and multiple sources of disadvantage requires marshalling know-how from several different sources and professions in a joint-effort, combining the tacit knowledge of people on the ground with the explicit skills of professionals. This is a central component in mutual approaches to community development and also in the most impressive credit unions.

Mutuals are ideally suited to deliver a joined-up approach to community renewal and to reinvigorate traditional public sector organisations. For example, under-performing schools have been turned around often by generating mutual commitment from parents, teachers, governors and local people. The most impressive examples of regeneration on housing estates involve people making mutual and complementary commitments to improve their neighbourhoods. Mutualism implies an active form of welfare in which the users and clients are partly responsible, as co-producers, for providing the services which they consume.

The relationship between the state and the mutual sector is critical. The state has progressively displaced mutuals in the twentieth century. As a regulator it has frequently played a critical role, tipping the balance in competition between mutuals and investor-owned companies. The prospects for mutuals will in part turn on public policy deicisions concerning them.

Mutual weaknesses

The core strength of a mutual is often also the source of its main weakness. Making the most of a membership base is time-consuming and difficult not just for managers but also for members, who have to make a commitment. Decision-making procedures to provide members with a tangible sense of membership are hard to devise and maintain. Membership organisations face two different problems. One is that their membership can become too large, dispersed and diverse to allow it to maintain a strong sense of common purpose: membership becomes diluted. The other problem is that a membership can become too closed, inward-looking and introverted. In those circumstances a mutual can easily ossify.

Membership-based organisations often thrive when their members come from a specific locality or occupation. The co-operative movement started with the Rochdale pioneers' belief in local, collaborative solutions to shared problems. The more dispersed a membership becomes, the more difficult it is to sustain a shared sense of belonging, although new technologies should make it easier to engage an active but dispersed membership. Dispersal makes it more difficult for members to monitor the performance of managers. When membership is small, close-knit, knowledgeable and trades with the mutual repeatedly – for example a small co-operative of farmers – its easy for the members to feel involved and for them to monitor the performance of managers. When a membership becomes much larger and more dispersed, when they trade with the mutual less frequently, members can become less knowledgeable, less involved and less able to keep a check on the managers.

Membership organisations thrive with a reasonable homogeneity of interest among its members. That is one reason why partnerships are so common in professions such as accountancy and law, where the partners have similar training and skills. The greater the diversity of interests within the membership the more difficult it is to sustain agreement on a common source of action. As a result mutual governance becomes more of a handicap than a help. A mutual thrives with a common purpose; with a more diverse membership a mutual can become confused by multiple and conflicting objectives. Often the way out is for mutuals to stress the lowest common denominator to bring together a large, diverse membership. In the case of large finance services providers, this common denominator might be simply the price and quality of service. But this can leave the service offered by a mutual looking indistinguishable from that provided by a private sector company.

A quite different problem is that a membership organisation can easily become exclusive and inward-looking, organised for current rather than potential members, insiders rather than outsiders.

Membership organisations with little new blood can become conservative. The membership base, which should be a source of innovation, defends the status quo. This creeping conservatism often afflicts worker co-operatives, which can quickly become captured by insiders who resist new ideas from the outside. Workers' co-operatives are frequently held together by egalitarian pay structures which dull incentives for people to come up with unsettling, innovative ideas. In these circumstances decline sets in.

Being a member has advantages but it also involves costs. When the costs of membership – financial costs as well as the time and energy required to be an active member – outweigh the benefits then members will desert mutuals for organisations which give them a better deal. A private sector company might charge a higher price for a service than a mutual but consumers are spared the costs and responsibility of being involved as a member.

Mutuals and co-operatives are commonly thought to suffer from another shortcoming: they find it more difficult to raise capital than investor-owned companies. This is one argument of those who advocate building societies should become shareholder owned banks. Goldman Sachs, the finance house, justified its decision to float on the stock market in part because its partners were unlikely to be able to raise the capital the company needed to compete in global markets. This problem is unlikely to be decisive. Henry Hansmann's comprehensive study of mutuality in the United States shows that mutuals are able to raise capital through borrowing and that there are many mutuals in capital-intensive industries.

Successful mutuals operate in a relatively narrow strip poised between two different threats. When their membership becomes too large, dispersed and diverse, the sense of membership they thrive upon becomes diluted. When the membership is too closed, stable and tightly-knit, a mutual can become conservative and inward-looking. Membership involvement in a mutual does not automatically confer upon the organisation the innovative capacity their advocates claim. Much depends on how mutuals are managed to make the most of their strengths, a feature born out in the case studies of successful mutuals in the next chapter.

3. Mutuals in Britain: an audit

In this chapter we assess the strengths, weaknesses, extent and prospects for mutual organisations across different sectors of the economy, examining the role of both established and innovative mutuals. One of the strengths of mutuals is their capacity to address several needs at the same time. A pre-school play group, for example, does not just deliver nursery provision but helps adults acquire skills and confidence and engenders a sense of community. As a result, it is sometimes difficult to fit a mutual into a particular sector and doing so may miss some of its most valuable attributes. We have looked at the strengths and weaknesses of mutuals in ten sectors of the economy serving some of our most basic needs:

- Childcare
- Education
- Housing
- Community development
- Crime prevention and community safety
- Health
- Financial services
- Employment
- Business
- Environment

3.1 Childcare

History and extent

The largest mutual providers of childcare are the 18,000 pre-school groups allied to the Pre-School Learning Alliance (formerly the Pre-School Play Groups Association.) Pre-school groups emerged in the 1960s, from a campaign among parents for state provision of nursery places. By 1998, there were 694,423 children under five-years-old attending pre-school groups, about 19 per cent of the under-fives; about 48 per cent of three to four-year-olds attended one of the groups.

Parents play an important role in the groups. About 1 million parents are involved in pre-school groups, helping to organise activities for children, fund-raising or managing the group. About three-quarters of pre-school groups are charities with parents represented on the management board. The groups use funds raised from fees, fund-raising events and donations to employ staff. pre-school groups also help parents gain skills: the Pre-School Learning Alliance provides training courses for 40,000 staff and parents a year. Many of the staff in pre-school groups are former parents; almost all are women.

Most of the rest of childcare for under-fives provided outside the family is delivered by local authority, private or workplace based nurseries as well as licensed day care providers.

About 1,500 pre-school groups have closed in the past two years. The Pre-School Learning Alliance argues this is because changes to government funding have encouraged primary schools to open large reception classes for three and four-year-olds. Parents keen to get their children into a primary school are under pressure to send their children to these nursery classes. The government has launched an inquiry into the factors behind the spate of closures among pre-school groups.

Strengths and weaknesses

Parental involvement in childcare gives these groups a cost advantage, which also makes the groups affordable for women on low incomes. School nurseries need only have one adult per thirteen children. Pre-schools must have one adult per eight children and in many there is one adult per six children. Staff in pre-school groups are invariably paid less than an equivalent teacher. The groups' informality makes them more approachable for parents who may feel put off by official public service procedures. Pre-school groups are able to get closer to their potential customers by using local knowledge and contacts. Parents benefit from their involvement: many have returned to education or acquired transferable skills which in turn have helped them to get jobs. The Pre-School Learning Alliance courses are a model for delivering uncertified adult learning to women, mainly in their thirties, many of whom left school with few qualifications and are starting to look for work. Pre-school groups help mothers to overcome isolation and can become a focus for a wider sense of community renewal: they help to bind a community together and give it confidence.

Critics of pre-school groups allege the educational quality of their provision is sometimes poor. To ensure pre-schools are up to scratch they are now inspected by Ofsted. This example, of submitting to external auditing, is something other mutuals will have to engage in if they are to be given a larger role in public programmes. Minimum wage legislation could force many pre-school groups to raise salaries which could price them beyond the reach of poorer parents. Shifts in education policy and growing competition from schools has exposed the limited strategic management capacity of local mutuals, which focus on keeping their heads above water, often in trying circumstances. This raises larger issues about how easily an infrastructure of local, self-governing mutuals can be strategically managed to meet new, more exacting, standards. A further problem is that it is difficult to quantify the added-value of a pre-school group in building community strength and parental capacity, other than through qualifications that parents gain.

Case studies
Marsh Lane Family Centre, Sefton
The Marsh Lane Family Centre started life in 1984 with a £17,000 urban programme grant to convert some garages on a run-down estate in Bootle into a home for a toddlers' group. Sandi Alexander who was employed to run the group recalls: 'There were rats running around and lots of cockroaches. We used to hear the whistles of people coming in taxis from the city to collect their drugs.' Most of the parents, often very young, were on their own, struggling with boisterous and difficult children while living on benefits.

Sandi Alexander encouraged parents to do more than simply drop their kids and run. The toddlers' group became a pre-school play group involving parents. Alexander's group became so successful at helping families with complex and compounded problems – family break-down, drug dependency, domestic violence – that it was funded as a family centre by Sefton social services, which eventually converted all its nurseries into centres modelled on Marsh Lane.

The Marsh Lane centre believes childcare should be provided in the community, by the community. Its aim is to support families, not simply to provide a service. Many families have stayed with the centre even after the children have gone on to secondary school. The Marsh Lane centre is an exemplary model of mutual self-help. It does not just provide a childcare service. The centre helps parents to understand and address all their child's needs; build their own skills as parents; and build lasting relationships with one another and the centre. As a result, it has become a focus for the community through which mothers can voice their views about crime, safety and the environment. Marsh Lane can go so much further than a traditional nursery because it is a mutual of parents.

First Steps Nursery, Twerton, Bath

The First Steps Nursery was set up three years ago in the middle of three large council housing estates on the outskirts of Bath. Twerton has the highest rate of drug-related crime in the country and one of the highest long-term unemployment rates in Europe. The number of children who 'fail' their developmental check at the age of three is twice the national average.

Pauline Hatherill, then an area organiser for pre-school groups, was alerted to the needs of young single mothers, many of them isolated and depressed, by a childcare teacher at a local secondary school. Hatherill did some market research and wrote a plan to create a family-centred nursery. She formed a steering group and raised £35,000 to convert a disused old people's home. The nursery is within the Sanctuary Housing Association Foyer project for young homeless people. Hatherill's philosophy is that parents should be the prime educators, children learn most through play and learning should be for life.

The nursery has eighteen staff and caters for 87 children every day of the week, from 8am till 6pm. More than two-thirds of parents are on state benefits and half the children are from single parent families. About 40 per cent of the children are judged to have special educational needs. Each child has a portfolio in which staff place examples of work, photographs of tasks completed and progress reports, which are updated every three months.

Parents, who are strongly represented on the management board and encouraged to be involved in all aspects of the nursery, get a written report twice a year and there are two open evenings. Sixteen parents have just completed an IT training course and several have gone on to further education. Forty-eight mothers involved in the nursery have completed courses and 35 have been helped into part-time employment.

The centre crosses every boundary between education, training, housing, health and social services. First Steps Nursery is based on sound economics but fragile finances. It costs about £150,000 a year to keep a child in residential care. If First Steps prevents two children a year going into care by helping their mothers cope with them, it would cover much of its running costs. Pauline Hatherill has twenty years' experience as a teacher but is paid only £13,000, the going rate for a probationary teacher. An Ofsted report found that all staff were paid well below the national average and they were 'constantly using their own resources to supplement materials and equipment'. The low costs are essential for First Steps to serve local mothers. Whereas the going rate for nursery care in Bath is £3.25 per hour, First Steps charges only £1 a hour for mothers on benefits and £2 an hour for those in a job.

Future prospects

In theory the prospects for pre-school groups should be promising, especially where they live up to their claims to help parents as well as children. They provide an excellent model for family learning centres, able to address the needs of families in a coherent and supportive fashion within the community. Pre-school groups excel at reaching isolated mothers with few qualifications who are often intimidated by official public services. They could thus also play a role in the government's lifelong learning programme.

However, to develop this potential many pre-school groups would have to upgrade their staff training and skills. The strength of self-help groups is their local knowledge; one of their weaknesses is their lack of strategic management and long-term development.

In reality, their future role will be heavily influenced by state funding and regulation of nurseries. The state is the mutual sector's main competitor. Schools have an incentive to expand nursery provision because the more children they recruit into nursery classes the more money they get. The Pre-School Learning Alliance argues the funding regime should provide stronger underpinning for the local, mutual infrastructure. One possibility would be for funding of nursery provision to be put in the hands of a special funding body, akin to that for further and higher education, which would be mandated to maintain a diversity of providers within an area.

3.2 Education
History and extent
Mutuals and co-operative organisations have long had a role in education. Trade unions and the Workers' Educational Association (WEA) have extended learning opportunities to members on a large scale since their foundation. The unions and WEA are seeking to develop their role in lifelong learning.

The WEA is the largest provider of further education courses in England and Scotland, with more than 650 member-run branches providing 10,000 courses, which in 1996–97 attracted 116,000 students. The University of the Third Age (U3A), a network of self-funded and self-managed organisations, offers courses for retired people: there are some 365 U3A branches in the UK with over 65,000 members.

Mutuals and co-operatives are marginal in the education system as a whole, which is dominated by public provision, especially among school-age children. Small schools, as promoted by Human Scale Education, offer an innovative way of running schools but are numbered in the dozens. Home education, which can sometimes be mutualist, accounts for 25,000 families according to the charity Education Otherwise. This represents less than 0.5 per cent of all school-age children.[9]

Other forms of mutualism include community centres that offer parenting education; tenants' associations' learning centres on social housing estates, such as the Community Learning Utility of the Swale Housing Tenants' Resource Centre; youth organisations such as the Guides and Scouts; parent–teacher associations (PTAs); a huge range of informal learning networks such as reading circles; experiential learning organisations such as Common Purpose, which runs mutual learning courses for professionals in different sectors in cities.

Strengths and weaknesses

The strengths of the unions and WEA derived from their capacity to tap large working-class populations with a desire for post-school learning. The WEA extended its reach well beyond the 'workers' and by the 1980s it had developed a middle-class image. In schools, mutuals are one way to involve parents more directly in their child's education, for example through a parent's group or PTA. Reforms to state education that seek to involve parents more in schooling will likely draw upon mutual models.

Mutual approaches also figure in innovative and experimental approaches to reach parts of the community ignored or alienated by mainstream education provision, yet unable to afford private education. Mutuals could play a role in promoting 'lifelong learning' in workplaces and communities, for example via the proposed Internet-based National Grid for Learning and the new University for Industry.

Mutual approaches have been marginalised in terms of funding and their share of school learning, where government policy has focused on expanding and improving state provision in an effort to drive up standards.

Case studies

Workers' Educational Association

If asked to identify the kind of organisation least likely to survive, let alone thrive, in the political and economic climate of education since the 1980s, you could be forgiven for pointing to the Workers' Educational Association. A voluntary body founded in 1903, with roots deep in the tradition of intellectual aspiration and self-improvement nurtured in early trade unions, the Labour Party and the co-operative movement, the WEA has all the attributes, on the face of it, of a cultural dinosaur.

Appearances are deceptive. The WEA is the biggest provider of further education funded through the government's Further Education Funding Council (FEFC). The WEA is our largest voluntary sector provider of adult education and, after weathering the many changes in further education funding and policy during the past twenty years, it is well placed to become a force in the development of lifelong learning in the UK.

The WEA is funded by central government and local authorities to supply further education. In 1997 it received over £7 million in FEFC grants and raised more than £6 million from other grants, tuition fees and charges. The association has received public funding ever since the 1920s but has retained an identity rooted in the voluntary sector and what its General Secretary, Robert Lochrie, describes as a 'co-operative ethic'. The WEA resists being labelled a 'college' and cannot be assimilated into mainstream public sector models of course design and delivery.

The WEA is a charity. It does not describe itself as a mutual or a co-op, yet it promotes a democratic and participatory approach to shared learning:

- Students are all members, involved in planning their own learning and choosing and running courses.
- The WEA makes use of students' life experiences: oral history and local community and workplace studies have a major role in many courses.
- The WEA seeks to reach people who have gained least from the school system and who want to learn more.
- The association works with people at risk of social disadvantage – the unemployed, disabled people, people in ethnic minority communities and people returning to study after a long break from formal education.

Anyone can join a WEA class, regardless of previous experience and qualifications, and everyone who attends a course becomes a WEA member, able to take part in running the branch. Branches are run by member committees and supported by the WEA's professional staff (full-time and part-time tutors and administrators).

The WEA has secured stable funding from the FEFC on the basis of organisational changes to ensure it can deliver the quality and consistency of teaching demanded. This example of management modernisation carries lessons for other mutual organisations, for it created some tensions between the national body's strategic aims and the relative autonomy of districts and local branches. Local groups tend to focus on the 'liberal education' tradition of non-vocational courses. They have often resisted pressures for more vocational courses. The future of the WEA, as with many mutuals, will turn on its continuing ability to combine the strengths of its local base – committed volunteer members, low costs, the ability to reach people alienated by mainstream institutions – with an ability to respond to demands for innovation to develop national programmes for lifelong learning.

Trade unions and lifelong learning

The opportunity for unions to renew their appeal based on lifelong learning was recognised by the TUC in its 1998 report, *Union Gateways to Learning*: 'Trade unions could help ignite a learning revolution in this country. They make up the largest voluntary organisation in Britain. TUC unions represent 6.75 million employees – all potential learners.'[10]

The report sets out a vision of 'a shared commitment' to lifelong learning investment by employers, employees and unions alike, underpinning a mutual responsibility for raising skills levels, employability and capacity for full participation in society. An ambitious new role for trade unions would be to model themselves as mutual educators, working in partnership with employers and the state to draw members into lifelong learning. One model for this partnership approach, which was brought over from the United States in the 1980s, is the Employee Development Assistance Programme, which is jointly run by unions and management at Ford UK. Several initiatives are developing unions as partners in lifelong learning.[11]

● Unison, the public services union, has created an Open College to give members the opportunity to re-enter learning and to obtain professional and higher education qualifications.

- As part of this service, Unison, working with the WEA, offers 'Return to Learn' courses for members who have low confidence in their ability to learn skills or gain qualifications. More than 1,000 members per year take part and over half go on to further education and training.
- The courses are supported by Voluntary Education Advisers, former students who act as mentors, reassuring and motivating people returning to study.
- The union has formed learning partnerships with 200 public sector employers.
- The DfEE Union Learning Fund (ULF) is designed to create partnerships for innovative workplace learning programmes between unions, employers, training and enterprise councils, and training providers such as colleges.
- In Lincolnshire, the AEEU and partners in education and engineering businesses are working on a pilot project ('Working Mentors for Young People') to link union members as personal mentors to disaffected young people.

The unions have a large membership base, which reaches many people who have been disaffected with the established education system. Their reinvigoration as mutual educators will only be possible if the unions invest more in learning and make learning a more central part of their bargaining and support work.

Human Scale Education

Human Scale Education (HSE) is a charity that helps to develop mutualist approaches to schooling – principally parent owned and run 'small schools' with an ethos that is at odds with that fostered by either the state or private sector, independent schools.

HSE has its roots in The Small School, a secondary school in Hartland, North Devon, which was set up by the environmentalist, author and teacher Satish Kumar to pioneer community-based education that would offer small classes and a democratic style of management, foster environmentalist values and focus on active learning and interpersonal development. The school, set up in the early 1980s, generated so much interest that HSE was established in 1986 to spread its approach elsewhere. HSE's has several core values:

- Small classes and a small-scale organisation make possible greater flexibility in the curriculum and more participation and democratic involvement of teachers, parents and pupils in working together and deciding how the school should develop.
- Schools need to help develop rounded character through greater integration of education in the life of the local community; active, participatory learning; and exploration of environmental values.
- Children should be treated as members of a community to which they have much to offer and in which they have a say.

HSE is in touch with 27 schools, including several for children with special needs, and also with the network of Steiner Waldorf schools (based on the teachings of Rudolf Steiner). Most are in rural or suburban areas and there is a middle-class bias in the movement, but there are some city schools, such as the Southwark Small School and a secondary school in Toxteth, Liverpool.

The schools range from ten or fifteen pupils to 50 or 60. There is an even mix of primary and secondary schools. Some have been set up from scratch and others are village schools that were taken over by parents to stop them from being closed down by local authorities as unviable. HSE believes parents are drawn to its schools by the sustainable environmental values they promote and also out of dissatisfaction with the inadequacies and rigidities of the state system, particularly for children with special needs. HSE argues there should be a growing role for an independent, social sector within education, which promotes diversity and choice within a national strategy for raising standards.

This embryonic mutualist movement in education faces many obstacles, including the lack of funding and critical mass. Yet the small schools help families and teachers feel part of the same venture and so offer one model for the renewal of the appeal of the state sector.

Future prospects
The government's lifelong learning agenda, the demand for innovation and modernisation in state education, the upsurge in interest within

business in organisational learning and the growing appeal of family and home-based learning will open up new possibilities for mutuals in education. For example, the scale and resources of the BBC could allow it to become the premier mutual organisation for learning over the Internet, in partnership with many different course designers and promoters such as the WEA. The BBC could be the basis for the largest 'learning club' in the world.

Older mutuals, such as the Workers Education Association, have survived in better shape than older mutuals in other sectors such as building societies and co-operative retailers largely because the WEA has negotiated a new partnership with the public sector that could be a model for public–mutual partnerships in other fields. Trade unions are, in principle, ideally placed to provide lifelong learning: much depends on whether they have the entrepreneurial leadership to take the opportunity.

The scope for creating mutual organisations within the secondary and junior school sector is limited by the predominance of public provision, with 'branded' private schooling as the main alternative. Yet many state schools are becoming more mutalist: they rely on a mutual organisation – a parent–teacher association – and parents now elect governors. One possibility, canvassed by Tom Bentley, is the creation of a parents' mutual which would extend beyond school governance and fund-raising to organise childcare and other family related services.[12] In many of the most innovative state schools – such as West Walker in Newcastle – mainstream educational services have been combined with social and environmental services, a healthy living centre and a housing project, and the schools are a focus for mutual self-help within the community.

3.3 Housing
History and extent
Housing lies at the foundation of the mutual movement. Building societies were born from self-build housing schemes in the eighteenth century. Yet mutuals were marginalised by the growth of council housing in the post-war era and, since the 1960s, the creation of a mass market in privately owned housing. Housing associations and other 'social landlords' including co-ops account for only 5 per cent of housing, or 1 million dwellings. Few housing associations are mutual

in any sense. The social housing sector is responsible for 15 per cent of new building, with the rest provided by the private sector.

These developments have left the classic forms of mutuality in housing – co-operatives social housing, self-build schemes and tenant management organisations – on the fringes of housing policy, despite their powerful claims as models that can generate benefits for the wider community as well as for tenants and owners.[13] Tenant management schemes, of which there are over 150 in the public sector managing some 57,000 homes, have often improved the quality of life on housing estates markedly. Co-ops make up 12 per cent of Registered Social Landlords (RSLs): in 1996 there were 259 fully mutual co-ops registered with the Housing Corporation, covering some 10,000 rented homes.[14] Community self-build schemes are thin on the ground: between 1990 and 1998, 60 projects were completed, and in June 1998 there were eighteen on site, twenty with funding allocated, and eighteen in the pipeline.[15]

A few housing associations, while not formally mutuals, have a mutual ethos: an example is the charity Anchor Trust, the UK's largest supplier of sheltered housing, the fourth biggest independent provider of home care, the largest non-profit residential care provider and the biggest home improvement agency. The trust has 10,000 staff and more than 55,000 customers. Anchor's success in operating across the boundaries of housing, health and social care in partnership with other agencies gives it a mutual self-help ethos, which will be reinforced by measures to improve customers' involvement in decision-making on issues affecting their quality of life.

Strengths and weaknesses

Mutual approaches to housing build links between self-management of housing estates and efforts to tackle related social issues of drug dependency, educational under-achievement and family breakdown. A Price Waterhouse report for the government showed that tenant management organisations 'were as cost-effective as the best mainstream social housing managers'; had lower operating costs than local authority providers; provided excellent maintenance and repairs services; and generated wider social benefits such as new skills development.[16]

Yet mutuals face several obstacles including:

- the decline of mutual building societies
- dependence of social housing associations on public money, which limits their scope for innovation
- the defensive and reactive nature of many tenants' associations
- alleged mistrust on the part of the Housing Corporation for of co-op schemes, and especially of the small-scale tenant management models that Price Waterhouse found worked best
- the marginal and exotic image of the self-build sector which has projects worth only £30 million under development.

Case studies
Community Self-Build Agency
The Community Self-Build Agency (CSBA), a voluntary organisation set up in 1989 with four staff, promotes and facilitates self-built housing for those in need. Inspired by a community self-build project in the early 1980s for excluded young black people in the St Paul's district of Bristol, the agency was formed by the Housing Corporation and Thames Telethon TV Trust. CSBA helps to match groups and projects to local partners and supports self-builders throughout the process. The agency's arguments for self-build emphasise the mutual benefits that extend beyond the provision of housing.

Self-build generates skills not only in building but also in project management, negotiation, consensus-seeking and communications, since self-builders must take a project from conception to completion and deal with a wide range of partners. Self-build is especially valuable in regeneration programmes that tackle social exclusion. As Anna McGettigan, the agency's director, puts it: 'Self-build only works if you learn how to work with a whole network of other people and organisations who you can go back to afterwards. It's broader access to other people that makes the difference.' Self-build schemes can generate enthusiasm within a community, foster co-operation and create a sense of common cause. These projects provide a setting in which confidence, skills and information can be transmitted rapidly and effectively.

Walter Segal Self-Build Trust
The Segal Trust charity specialises in promoting among people on low incomes and in housing need a building technique pioneered by its

inspiration, the community architect Walter Segal, who died in 1985. Segal developed an environmentally friendly and relatively simple form of dwelling design for easier building based on a timber frame, standard materials and modular design to avoid waste and to make alterations and extensions easy. The technique is recognised as one of the most environmentally sound and energy-efficient approaches to home construction. The cost of materials and fees for a Segal three-bedroom home (excluding land) is around £34,000; the average time taken to complete a self-build project of this kind is around 22 months. There are completed Segal developments in several cities and rural areas, and housing worth some £5 million was under development using the Segal method by summer 1998.[17] Segal scheme include self-built community centres as well as residential housing.

People attracted to community self-build schemes often feel hampered by the bureaucracy of housing associations and local authorities' housing departments, whose processes are not geared to self-build projects. The self-build sector is small and fragmented and self-builders often find it difficult to work with housing associations and their schemes, which usually cut across the official budget boundaries, often lack adequate funding.

The way ahead for this approach to community development, which has so much potential, lies partly in more effective collaboration between the self-build agencies. New forms of 'joined up' finance for community enterprise would help fulfil self-build's potential to meet not only housing need but also generate skills and confidence in communities. But perhaps the key to unlocking the potential of the sector's approach to mutuality would be a requirement for 10 per cent of all new social housing to be community self-build provision. This would reinforce the expertise of the existing agencies, attract new entrants and provide an incentive for housing associations to take the sector seriously as a major partner in 'Housing Plus' initiatives.

Tenants' co-operatives

The benefits generated by entrusting the management of social housing to tenants' co-operative organisations were highlighted by a detailed analysis by Price Waterhouse and backed up by other studies.[18]

The success of social housing schemes and urban regeneration

projects depends on their generating a sense of ownership and participation among residents. Examples abound of mutualist approaches to
involving tenants in the design, running and development of social
housing, which have created multiple benefits for local people. Some
are based on formal housing management co-operatives – tenant
management organisations (TMOs) – while others have developed co-
operation and mutual support between tenants and social landlords

An outstanding example of good practice against a backdrop of
social exclusion and long-term economic decline is the Eldonians
housing and regeneration association in Liverpool, which has developed high-quality housing for people on low incomes in a disadvantaged area of the city, as well as a village hall, sports and leisure facilities, education and training schemes and child care and crime prevention initiatives. The Eldonians began as a small co-op and, after
completing its first phase of social housing development, turned itself
into a community-based housing association aiming at the development of a sustainable and 'socially included' local community.[19]

In the past few years, local authorities and housing associations have
launched a range of initiatives to involve tenants, ranging from consultation with tenants, to tenant representation on housing management
teams and the creation of community development trusts to run social
housing on which tenants take up management positions. Full-scale
tenant control on co-operative lines usually depends on carefully
designed and delivered training to equip people with the skills and
confidence to take on the responsibilities of running a housing
mutual.

A key step towards tenant self-management is the formal recognition
of mutual rights and responsibilities between tenants and social landlords, for example in the shape of a 'community declaration' or mutual
plan for an estate. Such a declaration has been developed in the
Monsall district in Manchester. The agreement sets out what the
tenants and the landlord expect from the other in respect of the
management of the estate, provision and maintenance of facilities,
treatment of neighbours and the local environment. In Birmingham,
the city's 'Local Involvement, Local Action' programme aims to help
tenants take 'ownership' of problems and solutions. It allocates modest
discretionary budgets for neighbourhood improvements to 'ward advi-

sory boards' which develop spending plans based on neighbourhood strategies drawn up through local residents' forums. This kind of approach can help build up tenants' capacity to take on more ambitious roles in the management of social housing and Housing Plus regeneration strategies.[20]

The Co-operative Council's 1998 report, *Co-operative Housing: Realising the potential*, presents compelling case studies of fully-fledged social housing co-ops which underline the message of the 1995 Price Waterhouse report.[21] Some examples of how tenant-led co-operative approaches have a transformed social housing schemes are outlined below.

In Heath Town, Wolverhampton, tenant management co-ops have transformed the reputations of some of the hardest-to-let estates in the city after the local council decided in the early 1990s that progress would only be made with a tenant-led strategy for change. In 1996 the Heath Town Estate Management Board took over the management of 1,200 homes. The board is an elected committee of a co-op association for the area which is open to all residents. The benefits of the change in management have included: reductions in empty property, significant savings in repair costs, rental income from refurbished homes, security improvements and sports and leisure facilities.

The famous Coin Street social housing co-operative project was followed by the creation of a sister co-op, the Redwood Housing Co-operative at Oxo Tower wharf in London. Coin Street has attracted awards for showing how to create high-quality social housing in a central urban area dominated by business which would otherwise be too expensive for people on low incomes. The scheme was managed by Coin Street Community Builders, a partner to the Coin Street Secondary Housing Co-op. The Redwood organisation provides the same service as others in the Coin Street family of housing mutuals: affordable social housing for people in housing need who have a demonstrable need to live in the area, especially those in low-paid jobs with unsocial hours in central London who need to live close to their employment.

The Meriden Street Co-op in Coventry sprang from the resistance of residents in a home for people with learning difficulties to a city council proposal to close the building. With the help of the consultancy Partners for Change and numerous voluntary and public sector partners, the residents formed a co-operative association whose membership covers those living in the home and advisory members invited on board by residents. The creation of the co-op led to a new organisational structure, with the council leasing the building to the co-op which rents out rooms to members. The tenants select the staff and make their own management decisions through the general meetings attended by residents and advisory members who provide support over financial issues.

Lochfield Park co-op in Easterhouse, Glasgow, demonstrates how a tenant-led scheme in a deeply disadvantaged urban neighbourhood can achieve results that public sector – or business-dominated schemes – rarely bring about. The Lochfield Park Co-op owns and runs more than 400 homes in Easterhouse and works with Glasgow City Council and Scottish Homes to manage the estate. It has become a community regeneration mutual, developing initiatives to reduce local crime, running social activities, creating a park and developing community arts initiatives.

Tenants' co-ops have an impressive record. There is growing evidence that when they are backed by partners from the public, voluntary and private sector they can match the quality of housing management provided by traditional landlords. However, housing regulation favours large housing associations run by housing professionals, at the expense of smaller organisations that engage with local issues beyond housing, including crime, health, the environment and recreation. There is a powerful case for reform of the Housing Corporation's regulatory and performance measurement systems to give TMOs the larger role in housing management that their track record suggests they ought to have.

Future prospects
The case for innovative mutualist approaches to provision of private and social housing is very powerful. First, mutual, tenant self-management of housing estates has a significant role to play in neighbourhood renewal and 'joined up' initiatives to tackle social exclusion. Second, tenants of established social housing providers – housing associations and local authorities – want more choice and control over their

housing. Third, there will be a growing demand for affordable housing, often within cities, especially for single people and lone-parents on low incomes who may not be able to enter the private market.

But mutual approaches such as TMOs and self-build schemes are held back by several factors. Self build schemes need access to funding to ease start-ups and. Existing co-ops and self-build agencies need to collaborate more effectively. Above all, mutual approaches to social housing will only realise their potential with a supportive policy framework in which mutual approaches are enshrined as a mainstream choice for social housing and regeneration.

A first step would be to create 'public–mutual' partnerships, in which tenant and neighbourhood organisations take responsibility for the management of an estate. This mutualisation of social housing strategy should be a part of the government's strategy for neighbourhood renewal being drawn up by the Social Exclusion Unit and its New Deal for Communities.

Michael Young and Gerard Lemos recommend mutuality in housing be promoted by requiring social landlords to offer mutual aid agreements to residents in the form of Mutual Aid Compacts and to build in wider social criteria of willingness to provide mutual support into allocation decisions.[22]

There may also be opportunities to promote 'private–mutual' partnerships: forms of cooperative private ownership. The fastest growing form of housing provision in the United States is the condominium. In 1960, more than 99 per cent of residential apartments in multi-unit buildings were rented from commercial landlords. By 1991, co-operatives and condominiums – mutuals of private owners – accounted for 16 per cent of multi-unit housing. A similar growth in co-operative but private housing in the UK however would require legislation to create a new form of 'commonhold'. The government is committed to such a change but has yet to bring forward proposals.

3.4 Community development
History and extent
Community development initiatives that first began in the UK in the 1960s have grown rapidly in the 1990s, albeit from a small base. Many of these initiatives learn from the success of schemes in the United

States. There are 139 development trusts in the UK, with assets of £160 million, an annual income of about £30 million and about 18,600 members. They employ about 1,400 people and 1,110 volunteers, as well as 440 staff in their trading subsidiaries. Development trusts are non-profit making and managed with a degree of community membership to promote local economic, social, cultural and environmental regeneration. The trusts use donations and grants to acquire assets on the behalf of the community that can allow the trust to become self-sustaining: so-called asset-based development.

The first trust was set up in North Kensington in 1971 to develop land beneath the Westway, a raised carriageway. Almost three-quarters of the trusts have been created in the 1990s and 56 per cent since 1993. They cover a diverse range of communities, from former pit villages and areas of heavy industry to rural towns and coastal resorts. About 78 per cent of trusts open their membership to anyone living in the area where they operate and 64 per cent are open to people who work in the area.

The trusts undertake a wide range of tasks, from training, job creation and community safety to childcare, property development and arts schemes. They often act as bridges to the community for publicly funded regeneration schemes such as SRB partnerships and the New Deal.

The first community foundation was set up in Cleveland, Ohio in 1914 by a lawyer who wanted to create a tax efficient vehicle for local people to make donations to local charities. There are 500 community foundations in the United States with endowments of $13 billion and 90 in Canada with endowments of $1 billion. The first of the 42 British foundations was set up in 1986. By the end of 1999 there should be 54 foundations covering 60 per cent of the UK population. The foundations had an endowment of £65 million in 1997–98, an income from all sources of £30 million and made grants of £12.4 million. The Tyne and Wear Foundation has an endowment of £18 million and made 500 grants with a combined value of more than £1 million in 1997–98. Proctor and Gamble has initiated the largest corporate backed community foundation fund, with a pledge of £1 million.

There are five community loan funds. The best known is the Aston Reinvestment Trust, which aims to provide loans to viable local businesses and community projects that find it hard to raise loans from commercial banks but are not eligible for public funds. The British funds are modelled on the 46 community development loan funds in the United States, which have invested $350 million, created 60,000 units of low-income housing, helped to provide more than 12,000 jobs and attracted approximately $3 billion additional investment from public and private sources. Community foundations and loan funds are based on a membership structure, which involves local people in policy making.

In addition to these community development initiatives there are 65 settlements and social action centres in the UK with assets of about £13.4 million and income of about £17.6 million.

Strengths and weaknesses
Community development initiatives should galvanise local commitment, legitimacy and resources. People should be more willing to commit themselves to local causes so they can directly observe the benefits. Through local know-how and commitment, community funds should be able to leverage in other sources of finance. Community partnerships are increasingly seen as a vital component in publicly funded regeneration initiatives.

Yet there are limits to these community-based initiatives. People may doubt the capacity of local charities to deliver because they may lack financial clout or management skills. The donor base in poorer communities may be too small. Many of these schemes are still in their infancy in the UK although established indigenous models of best practice are developing.

Case studies
Sheffield Employment Bond
The Sheffield Employment Bond was developed by CityLife, the charitable arm of the Cambridge based Relationships Foundation, which is a church-linked think tank focused on rebuilding a sense of community within cities. CityLife is working with a wide range of partners in Sheffield, among them the South Yorkshire Community Foundation, Sheffield Enterprise Agency and Sheffield Community Enterprise.

The bond allows people in Sheffield to lend to a local fund which will reinvest in local projects. The capital raised by selling bonds to Sheffield residents – the target is £2 million – will be lent for the North British Housing Association, which will pay interest on the loan, which will be secured against their properties. The interest income will not go back to the bond-holders but will be invested in local job creation schemes, some of them run by the Sheffield rebuild project. Grants from the fund will attract matching investment from public and private sources for job creation projects. Midland Bank has agreed to be a partner investor and Bradford and Bingley Building Society will act as trustee of the received funds.

The organisers estimate the first round of funding could create 400 jobs. CityLife estimates that a £5,000 loan to the fund from a top-rate taxpayer will cost £195 a year for five years in interest foregone. Its research found that 57 per cent of relatively affluent people in Sheffield said they would consider buying a bond. At the end of five years the investor can either redeem the bond and take their cash out, roll over their loan or write it off by turning it into a donation.

Martin Clarke, project leader at the Relationships Foundation, said: 'We want to get the whole city involved in tackling its own problems and to take ownership of them, rather than waiting for the private sector or the government to sort them out.' CityLife has had expressions of interest from several other cities wanting to follow Sheffield's lead. NatWest already offers a community bond scheme in which people can lend money to capitalise regional charitable loan funds.

Aston Reinvestment Trust
Mutuality is central to the Aston Reinvestment Trust, which was created in June 1997 to bring to the UK lessons from community reinvestment in the United States, in particular the impressive community lending of the South Shore Bank in Chicago.[23] Aston Reinvestment Trust is a community reinvestment fund in an area badly hit by factory closures. It recycles local savings to viable voluntary sector schemes and local businesses that cannot raise mainstream finance. By the end of 1998, the trust had capital of £741,000; about £266,000 had been raised from members of the founding industrial and provident society, Art Share. NatWest and Barclays, the clearing banks, played a critical role in supporting the creation of the fund.

The trust, which aims to raise £3.5 million by the year 2000, lends to projects that have both an economic and a social pay-off. Adrian Cadbury, the trust's chairman explained:

This is a mutual investment society to provide capital for projects which contribute to the economic and social regeneration of Birmingham. The aim is to back projects which are not bankable in the normal way and to assist local people to take responsibility for helping themselves and their neighbourhood.

Communities That Care

Communities That Care is another community regeneration initiative borrowed from the United States but not one that raises money. The idea, which is being piloted in Swansea, Coventry and Barnsley in a £1.3 million programme funded by the Joseph Rowntree Foundation, is to help communities assess their own strengths, weaknesses and risks particularly where young people are concerned.

The initiative stemmed from social scientists in the United States who, over several decades, had established the general 'risk factors' that were most associated with teenage pregnancy and young people becoming involved with crime, drugs and truancy. The 'risk factors' include family conflict, poor parental supervision, poor housing, low achievement in early schooling, poor school management, poor local amenities for young people, a high turnover of tenants and so on. There was no bridge to make this academic know-how available to community leaders trying to tackle these issues on the ground. Communities That Care, as with other mutuals such as pre-school groups and credit unions, aims to blend the formal know-how of experts with the on-the-ground knowledge of communities.

In Communities That Care, a project leader brings together community leaders including politicians, council officials, school governors, youth workers, police officers and community leaders to commission a risk audit of the neighbourhood, drawing on national statistics and an opinion survey of secondary school pupils. Using this data, the community management board, which in Barnsley involved about 80 people in its first meeting, assesses the risks and the community resources available to tackle them. That leads to a plan for action, informed by an analysis of promising approaches that have already been tried successfully elsewhere, for example support programmes for isolated single parents, family literacy schemes, after school clubs.

Future prospects
The prospects for the community development movement, particularly its most recent wave – development trusts, community foundations, city bond schemes and reinvestment loan funds – are promising. The movement is starting from a low base but is one of the fastest growing parts of the mutual sector and its is developing its own impressive models of best practice.

Government policy is supportive. A rising proportion of public funding channelled through the Single Regeneration Budget and the New Deal requires local partners to involve community groups. These schemes respond to a widely felt need for trustworthy vehicles for people to reinvest in the development of their localities. They provide a channel not just for money but also for professional expertise to be married with local know-how. Much will depend, as with other social and community mutuals, on whether the public sector and mutuals can develop a more creative and productive relationship.

3.5 Crime prevention and community safety
History and extent
The idea of informal 'neighbourhood policing' rooted in mutuality is part of the modern folklore of lost community. In the course of the past few decades crime prevention and community safety have been taken over by an increasingly professionalised police force – and at the same time they were privatised: they became a matter of individual risk management and security. Mutualism in crime prevention and community safety is now being rediscovered thanks to two factors.

First, there is dissatisfaction with traditional policing in the light of rising crime and fear of crime: the clear-up rate for crime is poor and fear of crime has grown, even if it is not borne out by statistics. Second, policy-makers recognise the connection between crime and social exclusion. Crime prevention needs to be devised in conjunction with community based measures to respond to bullying, family breakdown, disaffection from school, homelessness and school exclusion.[24]

The most common mutual crime prevention schemes are the 120,000 Neighbourhood Watch schemes which cover 5 million homes, about 25 per cent of the population. Some 20,000 of these schemes include a Street Watch element, including for example escort services for older people.

The more than 150 mediation initiatives helping people find shared solutions to local problems, are another example of mutualism.[25] These initiatives in 'restorative justice' cover mediation of neighbour disputes, victim–offender meeting and mediation, and conflict resolution in schools, environmental policy and other areas.

There are 250 crime prevention and community safety partnerships that bring together a range of actors in a neighbourhood to foster community safety. These partnerships have been carrying out audits of crime and safety in preparation for the launch of three-year plans for community safety.

Strengths and weaknesses
The failure of traditional remedies has fuelled the search for innovative solutions that can make a lasting difference to community safety by drawing on the motivation and know-how of local people. Community-based approaches can deliver an early warning that young people are at risk of becoming involved in crime, for example, whereas the police usually get involved only once a crime has been committed.

But community crime prevention demands a shift in attitudes among police and other professionals who are often unwilling to co-operate fully with community bodies. Jon Bright identifies a number of problems, including lack of clear goals, lack of coherent work plans and confusion as to the division of labour between different agencies.[26]

Other problems include a common mistrust among citizens and police, based on fears of vigilantism. Most Neighbourhood Watch schemes are not linked to deeper and wider community initiatives to promote early warning and prevention and social inclusion. Neighbourhood Watch works best where there is a strong sense of community. In disadvantaged areas, trust among residents and with the police and social services is often at a low ebb, which makes effective mutual aid schemes difficult to establish.

Case studies
Balsall Heath Community Forum: Street Watch Initiative

Raja Amin and his neighbours in the Balsall Heath district of Birmingham have been seen during the last few years successively as: subversive vigilantes by the police; unwelcome opponents by local criminals; community heroes by their neighbours and exponents of leading practice in mutual initiatives for community safety by local service providers, national politicians and the European Commission.

Raja, a local trade union official, chairs the Balsall Heath Community Forum, a community-owned and run association of residents, which has developed a wide range of linked projects for local economic and social regeneration. The forum was instrumental in fostering a sense of hope in the run-down district of Balsall Heath by developing with residents projects for environmental regeneration and job creation, with funding from the European Union. However fear of crime was a persistent problem, especially in relation to prostitution and kerb-crawling. In 1989, some 450 prostitutes and their pimps were a focus for related street and drug-related crime.

In 1995 the area formed the first urban Street Watch scheme, setting up daytime and nightly patrols with groups of six volunteers who established a peaceful presence on the streets that was sufficiently prominent to confront pimps and deter much criminal activity. The process was risky and controversial: Raja Amin and his colleagues were threatened by criminals and treated with suspicion by the police. They faced apathy and fear from some residents, many of whom felt the problem was too deep-rooted to be tackled by a self-help venture. There were also concerns about vigilantism and threats to civil liberties which were gradually overcome as the police and other stakeholders such as church representatives were won over by the evidence of the scheme's success and sensitivity to their anxieties.

The scheme eventually drove down crime and fear of crime, and gained the backing and then the support of the police and local authority. Advocates of the scheme argue prostitution has not been displaced but genuinely dispersed and deterred.[27] A police representative sits on the forum and his liaison work, backed by senior officers, was vital in building trust in the Street Watch. The police recognise the initiative relieves pressure on the police service and creates a recruiting ground for special constables and police officers.

Youth Works

Mutuals can play an equally important role in preventing young people becoming involved in criminality.[28] Jon Bright highlights the role of youth schemes which prevent truancy; reduce school exclusions; promote parental interest in school; prevent bullying; broaden the curriculum and encourage more peer education.[29]

Youth Works is an innovative programme aimed at fostering skills and combating disaffection among young people living in 'high risk' areas. Youth Works, which is run by the charity Groundwork in partnership with Crime Concern and Marks & Spencer, focuses on those aged eight to 25 on high-crime estates in deprived areas. The scheme involves young people in measures to improve their estate and so gives them a chance to develop skills by participating in schemes to reduce crime. Youth Works projects are running in Blackburn, Hackney, Leeds, Plymouth and Sunderland, involving local authorities, businesses and community organisations.

Work in Hackney, for example, has included the creation of a mural and new garden on one housing estate. Youth Works carried out a local community safety audit in the Haggerston area and its programme is to form the centrepiece of a strategy to involve young people in create recreation facilities on their estates. Youth Works will be linked with other youth programmes, environmental improvement plans and crime prevention schemes, such as Hackney's Dalston Youth Project, which provides fifteen to eighteen-year-old offenders with residential courses, training programmes and adult mentoring to ease them away from involvement in crime.

The Youth Works estate in Blackburn has seen a significant fall in vandalism: in two and a half years juvenile crime fell by more than a third, and in one twelve-month period estate management costs fell by more than a half as a result of the decline in vandalism. Criminal damage in the Youth Works estate in Sunderland fell by 66 per cent after the project got going.

The related Youth Project in Dalston has been judged by its evalua-
tors to be highly effective at motivating at-risk young people to take
part in further education, training and work, cutting the amount of
youth crime, re-offending rates and criminal damage costs, and
encouraging members of the wider community to tackle youth crime.
The mentoring process which is central to the project has created
numerous benefits for the mentors and peer tutors – new skills, greater
self-confidence and pride in the community.

The potency of this kind of approach to crime prevention is also
shown by another Crime Concern partnership, the Youth Action
groups set up by Crime Concern and Prudential plc. Pru Youth Action
is an initiative which has developed since 1993 into a national network
of 1200 groups involving some 20,000 young people in a quarter of all
secondary schools in the state sector. The initiative has attracted
support from government, police and local authorities. Youth Action
groups are designed to give young people a major role in projects to
prevent crime and bullying by involving them in running projects
such as community crime audits or school surveys and in organising
groups and meetings, and by treating them as 'essential partners in
community safety'.[30] Evaluation in 1997 indicated that the initiative
was succeeding in many areas in attracting support from young
peopl,e schools and the police, and that it was helping to develop skills,
self-esteem and confidence among those young people taking part, as
well as generating projects which helped reduce crime, bullying and
fear of crime and violence.

Initiatives such as these can work impressively, but require a well-
designed framework of support from co-operating agencies in the
public, private and voluntary sectors. Organisations in diverse policy
areas (crime, employment, education, regeneration) need to work to a
common agenda and commit themselves to a genuine partnership
with each other and with people in communities where crime and fear
of crime have become deep problems. Mutual projects in this area
demand patience and sustained effort over a long period: reducing
crime and fear of crime by boosting young people's sense of responsible citizenship and participation in the local economy and community
is a long-term strategy.

Future prospects
Mutual initiatives in crime prevention and community safety have huge potential. To make a major impact action on a larger scale would be needed in all local authority areas. Mutuals for crime prevention will only succeed on a large scale if they can win the trust and co-operation of police, social services and other voluntary groups. As with mutuals in other sectors they have to show how formal professional skills of police and social services can be combined with community involvement to generate more effective solutions to local problems. Three complementary initiatives should be taken:

(i)   Neighbourhood Watch needs to be developed to grow more Street Watch schemes and to link Neighbourhood Watch with wider community crime prevention initiatives. This would integrate Neighbourhood Watch more effectively into local strategies and spread knowledge of local 'risk' factors such as the Communities That Care programme.
(ii) 'Public–mutual' partnerships along the lines of the Balsall Heath project would develop a more effective division of labour between local community initiative and know-how, and the professional skills and knowledge of the police.
(iii) Bottom-up community crime initiatives need to be an integral part of community regeneration programmes funded by the New Deal for Communities or SRB programmes. In particular, these should develop ways to involve young people in designing and delivering local projects.

3.6 Health
History and extent
Since the establishment of the National Health Service in 1948, health policy has focused on the NHS's resourcing and internal organisation. Self-help and mutual provision, delivered by co-ops and friendly societies, was undermined by the development of national insurance and the state sector.[31] On the face of it the mutual sector seems marginal to healthcare.

However, this is a partial picture. Non-profit, independent providers are a minority in the hospital sector, yet they account for a significant share of acute care and elective surgery. Self-help and informal co-operative provision are central to long-term care. A vast informal sector of family care – largely individualised and fragmented – cares for disabled relatives, the elderly, sick children and mentally ill relatives. Some 5.7 million adults are unpaid carers: 'this is a vast ... resource of mutual aid, largely hidden and taken for granted'.[32] The informal care 'sector' provides services that would cost the state some £30 billion per year.

Non-profit organisations are significant providers of residential care. This growing market, worth some £8.5 billion, has been highly competitive since the large-scale contracting out of residential care from the public sector began in the 1980s. More than half this market is accounted for by the private sector but much of the rest is taken up by voluntary sector providers, a minority of which are mutuals or co-ops. In the domiciliary care sector, which is funded mostly by the NHS and local authorities, a recent study found there were 49 non-residential care co-ops in the UK, accounting for just over 1 per cent of the market.[33]

Co-operative approaches are more common in preventive and community health. Loughborough University researchers reported in 1996 that there were at least 300 community 'well-being' centres and co-ops in health and social care in England and Wales.[34]

Finally, self-help groups have blossomed, pooling information, lobbying for resources, matching specialist support to individuals and families, and acting as a focus for research into particular medical conditions or other health problems. One estimate is that there are perhaps between 2,000 and 3,000 such groups in the UK. One of the most important examples is the mutual support group umbrella body Contact a Family which works with around 1,000 local and 300 national self-help groups.

Mutuals also play a vital role in financing health care. In 1996–97 about 6 million people (about 10 per cent population) were members of cash benefit schemes. HSA, the largest scheme, accounts for about 50 per cent of the cash plan market. Many friendly societies run health cash plans. In addition there are about 40 city-based mutual health benefit funds.

Strengths and weaknesses
The scope for mutual provision will be largely determined by government policy. Mutual organisations are playing a larger role in part thanks to reforms introduced by the last Conservative government, which encouraged contracting out. In the future, mutual approaches may be encouraged by the government's stress on public health and preventive strategies linked to community renewal.

Mutuals tap discontent with both public and private provision. Many people find state provision too inflexible and slow, yet few can afford and many feel uneasy about using private services. Mutuals fit into the government's strategy to shift the emphasis of health policy towards improving public health and tackling health inequalities. This will mean linking health services to community initiatives that focus on, for example, primary care services, access to fresh food, health education, local environmental improvements, improved housing quality and so on.

The preventive focus is central to 'healthy living centres', which embody a mutualist philosophy. Mutual organisations have developed in the self-help care sector precisely because they create and share knowledge by connecting people in ways that public and private sector bodies find hard to replicate. These exemplify the capacity of mutuals to pool, share and create knowledge. Opportunities to gather and share knowledge are expanding, partly due to the amount of medical information available on the Internet, making mutualism more effective and rewarding. People find mutual self-help more friendly, reassuring and supportive than relying solely on professionals.

Yet mutuals face significant problems and shortcomings. Competition from the private sector is fierce in the residential and domiciliary care market. As in policing and education, mutuals in this sector face suspicion from professionals in social services and the NHS.

Case studies
Contact a Family
Contact a Family (CaF) has its origins in a dissatisfaction with public and private health services. Care services recognised the needs of children with disabilities and rare medical conditions but often did not

acknowledge the impact of their condition on their families. Many parents felt isolated, poorly informed and under strain.

CaF, founded in 1974, is a charity that meets the needs of such families for support and information by putting them in touch with others in the same situation and helping them form their own local or national mutual support groups. CaF co-ordinates a widening network of more than 1,000 local and more than 300 national support groups. There is a sister organisation in the United States and a European register of groups is being compiled. CaF has a small national office and is setting up regional offices to facilitate consultation with local groups.

CaF is not formally a mutual. But its chief executive Harry Marsh recognises its networks are based on a 'genuine mutual spirit' that encourages autonomous groups to come together to help themselves. New groups can affiliate to the CaF network by paying a nominal fee: after four years of membership a group gains full voting membership rights. There is a national annual conference and regular consultations at local and regional level with groups on policy positions and proposed initiatives. CaF is a lesson in involving people in mutuals: bureaucracy is kept to a minimum; many of the groups are 'kitchen table' organisations which do not have the time or resources to deal with paperwork.

The family support groups focus on particular disabilities and medical conditions – many of them very rare. CaF provides information about children's disabilities and special needs; it puts families in touch with other families and self-help groups; it acts as a facilitator and trainer for people wishing to set up new groups; and it provides advocacy and policy support for groups campaigning for resources or policy changes. CaF also helps groups negotiate more productive relationships with professionals in the field.

CaF is not free from tensions. Self-help groups have great strengths but also limits that are important to recognise. Activists frustrated by the scale of unmet need they face sometimes want their groups to become direct service providers. CaF advises groups to focus on a manageable workload rather than be tempted to extend their activities over-ambitiously and take on staff, which would require them to become far more formal.

Bromley-by-Bow Healthy Living Centre

The innovative community centre at Bromley-by-Bow is becoming a mecca for social entrepreneurs. The centre is a multi-purpose community enterprise in one of Britain's most deprived districts, running a wide variety of projects linking environmental improvements with schemes for skills development and education, or arts and sports work, to measures to counter disaffection and exclusion among young people.

The centre hosts the country's first healthy living centre, which links an array of primary care services to other initiatives to improve community quality of life. The government envisages a national network of such centres, partly funded from the Lottery.

The prototype healthy living centre was the Peckham Pioneer Health Centre, used by nearly 1,000 families before and after the Second World War. Peckham's centre was a charity run as a local health organisation that integrated primary care, social care and community activities.[35] Peckham's Pioneer Centre has inspired several community health projects, developed and run by volunteers and community workers rather than by mainstream professionals, who have largely remained wedded to the hierarchies and departmental boundaries of public sector organisation.

The Bromley-by-Bow Healthy Living Centre (HLC) was set up in 1997 on the Bromley 'campus' and is the first example of a community organisation taking responsibility for the design, construction and ownership of a health centre. Funding was secured from the local health authority and a mortgage serviced by rent from the GPs who have taken part of the building. The HLC offers not just clinical care but also a set of services to contribute to preventive programmes and wider community well-being. The building is a high-quality work of architecture, with extensive use of hand-made bricks and natural wood; it contains many works of art and is set in its own garden; its services provide opportunities for employment and counselling. The holistic vision is embodied in the primary care team, which includes not only six GPs but also other health workers, youth and family workers, and complementary therapists. Patients are likely to be offered 'treatments' which are a far cry from the standard prescription – singing lessons for asthmatics, dancing classes for the overweight, community projects and skills development for people unemployed through health problems.[36]

Benenden Healthcare Society

A more venerable and conventional form of health care mutuality are the friendly societies. Benenden Healthcare, established in 1905 as the Post Office and Civil Service Sanatorium Society, is a traditional mutual health society that serves members who have been employed in the Post Office, Civil Service and British Telecom, along with a number of associated bodies.

Benenden sees itself as a complement to the NHS, offering services for which there is a long wait on the NHS but which are expensive in the private health sector. It focuses on non-emergency hospital care, with a special cancer-care support service aimed at patients' families as well as the cancer sufferers. The service includes the arrangement of specialist consultations. Members pay 60 pence per person per week. The mutual ethos is reflected in its policies: there are no exclusions for pre-existing conditions and no increase in contributions with age.

The society is governed, says its Finance Director Michael Higgins, by 'activists with a strong mutual ethos'. There are some 80 branches to which new members are allocated and these send delegates to the biennial conference, which elects members of the Committee of Management. As in financial mutuals, there is considerable apathy about the democratic dimension of membership. Members are attracted by the service offer. The society grew its membership by 7 per cent in 1998 and there are some 970,000 people on cover, of which about 370,000 are members.

Benenden faces growing competition from the private sector, which is raising expectations among members of a more demand led approach. Michael Higgins, its finance director, acknowledges the mutuals must respond by becoming more innovative and flexible without compromising their mutual culture. Benenden has reorganised itself, moving from 'management by activists' to 'governance by activists'. Operational control has passed to a professional management team to improve efficiency and comply with the demands of the Friendly Societies Act, and to take a more proactive approach to marketing and service development.

Future prospects
The public sector will continue to dominate health care provision, but mutuals could play a larger role, either in partnership with the state – delivering or complementing state services – or in response to the failure of public services to meet diverse demands. Numerous opportunities for mutual approaches are opening up.

Healthy living centres that link preventive programmes to community renewal will depend on generating a mutual ethos. Public health is not a service that can be delivered by professionals; public health has to be created or produced by people in a locality. The consumers of public health – the public – also need to be among its 'producers'. That is why a mutual approach makes sense.

HLCs need to find an existing, trusted community 'hub' around which they can cluster: this is the strength of Bromley-by-Bow. HLCs should be based on 'campuses' such as that developing around West Walker Primary School on Tyneside, which plans to link an HLC to its community education services.[37]

Mutuals will play a growing role in knowledge creation and sharing about health, enabling people to take more charge of their care, often helped by the spread of easily accessible medical information on the Internet. The government's recognition of the role of informal carers through its New Deal for Carers could open up funding and a framework within which such networks and also care co-operatives could flourish.

3.7 Financial services
History and extent
Mutuality has its origins in co-operative savings and insurance schemes. In Roman times, 'collegia' helped their members to cope with sickness and to pay for a decent burial. In Medieval times, guilds helped to insure their members against unemployment, ill health and periods of hardship. The sickness and burial clubs which evolved after the guilds disbanded became friendly societies. These emerged in modern form in a burst of social and financial innovation in the final quarter of the eighteenth century. Equitable Life launched the first modern mutual life assurance scheme in 1762. Richard Ketley set up the first building society in Birmingham in 1775. Friendly societies were regulated under the Friendly Society Act of 1793.

In the nineteenth century, friendly societies were the only way workers could protect themselves against loss of income. At their peak there were perhaps 30,000 registered societies, covering more than half the working population. Even in the twentieth century, friendly societies played a critical role, distributing state sickness benefits. Only when the state took over that function in 1948 did friendly societies, which then had about 14 million members and 18,000 branches, go into decline. The number of societies fell from 2,740 in 1945 to 293 in 1998.

In the 1990s mutual financial services providers have found their market and their organisations under attack from shareholder owned banks rather than the state. In the mid-1990s a wave of 'de-mutualisation' among building societies and, to a lesser extent, mutual insurers converted historic mutuals into shareholder owned companies. The members of these societies received large windfalls in the process and many of the executives large share options.

Despite the decline of the mutuals from their peak they still play a critical, albeit smaller, role in financial services.

Building societies. The 70 mutual building societies had 2.8 million borrowers, 19 million investors and 37,309 employees at the end of 1997 and accounted for 17 per cent of retail deposits (£98.6 billion) and 23 per cent of outstanding residential mortgages (£105.34 billion), down from 80 per cent five years ago. Since the late 1980s a large number of the largest building societies have converted themselves into banks or been taken over by a bank. These included the Abbey National, the Halifax (the largest mortgage lender), the Cheltenham and Gloucester (bought by Lloyds), the Woolwich and the Alliance and Leicester. Eight of the ten largest building societies ten years ago are now banks. In April 1999, members of the Bradford and Bingley, the second largest building society, voted to convert the society into a bank.

Regulatory requirements designed to ensure lenders have a healthy balance sheet make it virtually impossible to create a new building society from scratch. The only building society to have been created in recent years is the Ecology Building Society, set up in 1981 and dedicated to building projects which follow ecological principles. It has assets of £22 million and loans outstanding of £17 million.

Mutual insurers. Some of the largest insurers are mutuals designed to benefit policy-holders. Standard Life, for example, is the largest mutual life assurance company, with assets of £50 billion, about £60 billion under management and 4 million customers. The mutual insurers, which include Equitable Life, Friends Provident, Scottish Life, Scottish Widows and the Royal London, took 27.2 per cent of the new yearly premiums market in 1991 and 22.7 per cent of new single premiums.

The Cooperative Insurance Society, which is wholly owned by the Cooperative Wholesale Society, has 3 million family customers, an annual turnover of about £2 billion and manages investments for customers worth about £17 billion. It made a surplus of £677 million in 1997.

Friendly societies. There are 293 registered friendly societies, which together have assets of about £12 billion. Friendly societies handle a large amount of mutual insurance for sickness, unemployment and retirement as well as life assurance. The 80 leading friendly societies that are members of the Association of Friendly Societies have £11.43 billion under management, 11.1 million policies, 4.76 million members, an income of £2.849 billion and pay annual benefits worth £867.6 million. The largest societies are the Liverpool Victoria with 1.5 million members and the Royal Liver, with 1 million.

Credit unions. Credit unions are well established in Ireland, where they cover 40 per cent of the population, and the United States, where there are 12,000 credit unions with assets of $316 billion and 70 million members. Credit unions are local savings and loan banks, which usually start by lending small sums. In the United States in 1998 credit unions accounted for 2.2 per cent of residential mortgages, worth $30 billion. The average credit union mortgage was $88,700, compared with $130,000 for other mortgage lenders.

A credit union has to be based around a 'common bond', normally either a workplace or a community. Credit unions only got started in the UK in the 1960s but have enjoyed strong growth, at least in numbers, in the 1990s. Between 1992 and 1997, the number of credit unions rose from 383 to 584, the number of members went up from 88,007 to 214,660 and the savings they handled rose from £28.5

million to £105.8 million. There were 447 community credit unions, with 108,000 members, loans outstanding of £24.7 million and assets of £36 million. The 83 workplace credit unions had 107,000 members, loans outstanding of £72.8 million and assets of £86.3 million. Many community credit unions are small, fragile and have found it difficult to grow. Community-based credit schemes are common in the Afro-Caribbean and Pakistani communities.

Microfinance. Mutual guarantee societies are commonplace in continental Europe, bringing together small businesses to provide collateral for one another and allowing them to borrow more cheaply. These societies are estimated to have advanced loans of £50 billion to small businesses in continental Europe. Eight mutual guarantee societies, with 260 small business members, are being piloted in the UK. In addition a group of social investors and community loan funds are creating the Rebuilding Society Network, with the ambitious aim of providing microfinance to 100,000 very small businesses by the year 2007.

Social banking. The Co-operative Bank, which is wholly owned by the Co-operative Wholesale Society, made a pre-tax profit of £55 million in 1997, up from £17.8 million in 1993; operating income was £316 million, up from £227.7 million in 1993. Bad debt charges were £26.3 million about 1.1 per cent of customer lending. The Co-operative Bank's return on equity was 23.6 per cent.

The Triodos Bank, a European social investment bank, opened in the UK in 1995. It has UK assets of £52 million and loans outstanding of £27 million. Triodos adopts a community approach to lending, for example encouraging communities to provide mutual guarantees for loans.

Strengths and weaknesses
Established mutuals – building societies, mutual insurers and friendly societies – are still large players in the financial services, albeit much less significant than they used to be. The remaining mutuals have responded to the competition by improving services, cutting costs and making more of the benefits of mutuality by providing a member dividend in the form of better rates than shareholder-owned mortgage

providers. The big wave of demutualisation in building societies has probably passed. The Nationwide, the largest building society, fought off two an attempts to convert it into a bank in 1997 and 1998. The remaining building societies have more effective defences against carpet-bagging.

The mutuals face a financial services industry which is consolidating into larger groups in search of economies of scale and lower costs. This cost competition will put a further squeeze of medium-sized mutuals to lower costs or improve their marketing and branding to make more of their mutual character. This may require mutuals to band together to access capital markets. Although the mutuals face an uncertain future, so does most of the rest of the financial services industry.

Credit unions highlight the potential and the obstacles faced by new mutuals. Credit unions are the fastest growing part of the new co-operative and mutual movement. Yet most community-based credit unions are struggling to survive. One strength of community based credit unions should be their local knowledge, which should allow them to identify bankable people and businesses that large banks might overlook. Community credit unions should also be more approachable than banks: they market themselves by word of mouth and generally adopt a more flexible and empathetic approach to bad loans. As they rely on members to provide services as volunteers, the credit unions should have lower costs than many banks.

These qualities – their access to local tacit know-how, their low costs and trustworthy reputation – should, in theory at least, allow community credit unions to play an important role in tackling financial exclusion, where they have a big market to aim at. Between 6 and 9 per cent of the population have no current or savings bank account, 50 per cent of the poorest families have no home contents insurance and 3 million people use the services of registered money lenders, who lend at APR rates of between 100 per cent and 500 per cent.

Yet community credit unions, despite their rapid growth, seem unlikely in their present form to become significant community-based providers of financial services. Despite support from perhaps 150 local authority credit union development agencies, with funding of close to £10 million a year and a flow of grants and public subsidies, only a handful of the 447 community credit unions are prospering, according to a detailed analysis by John Moore's University in Liverpool. The report found that only 4 per cent of the community credit unions were financially self-sufficient and 40 per cent had not reached the most basic level of economic viability, even though two-thirds of them were more than three years old.[38] Of community credit unions, 297 had fewer than 200 members and on average they had just 36 loans outstanding. These credit unions are unlikely to enter the virtuous circle credit unions need to prosper, in which they attract more members, make larger loans and so attract more members.

Community credit unions exemplify many of the difficulties of pursuing a deliberate policy to establishing mutuals. Eight out of ten community credit unions were started at the prompting of the local authority. They were not created by the community, for the community; so they lack the commitment that community voluntary organisations need to prosper. Workplace credit unions are based on a clear common bond and a readily organisable membership. Community credit unions lack that clarity of purpose and sense of belonging.

Nor do they have the professional, entrepreneurial management needed to succeed as competitive providers of financial services (almost 50 per cent of credit unions said they did not need a basic business plan to succeed.) Most rely on volunteers to make them work, which means two-thirds were open for six hours or less a week. That makes them inaccessible and so not particularly useful in tackling financial exclusion. As a result, most community credit unions make a negligible contribution to community economic development and tackling social exclusion. They are often seen as a second-best, poor person's bank; poor people say they want access to mainstream financial services.

These weaknesses are compounded by the fragmentation in the national leadership of the credit union movement, which has two national organisations. This underlines the difficulties of strategic management to upgrade the capabilities of a highly federated movement of independent mutuals. Their sense of local independence can be a weakness as well as a strength.

Case studies
Speke Community Credit Union
The woman was distraught. Her newborn baby had just died. She could not afford to bury her. The funeral would cost £300, a sum well beyond the reach of an unemployed single mother with several children. In despair she turned to the only credit available to her, a loan shark. She got the £300 she needed to bury her child. The loan shark made her pay £1,500 over the following months to clear the loan.

It was this woman's story that persuaded Mike and Doreen Knight that the community of Speke, on the outskirts of Liverpool, needed something different. By dint of their determination and energy, local know-how and entrepreneurship, the Knights, aided by a small army of helpers, have created one of Britain's most impressive community credit unions, at the heart of one of the country's most neglected housing estates.

The Speke Community Credit Union, has 1,500 members and it's recruiting 50 members a month by word of mouth. It is the only financial institution serving an estate of 6,000 homes and 13,000 people, on the periphery of Liverpool. People who could afford to moved out long ago. Unemployment is a condition of life for many on the estate. Some of the men work in the cash-in-hand economy of mini-cabs and window rounds. Many of the women are single mothers, with several children, often caught between the dole and the loan shark.

The last bank serving Speke, the TSB, closed its doors two years ago. The credit union occupies its former offices in the run-down shopping parade. Even if there were a bank in Speke most of the people would not be allowed an account, let alone a loan, insurance or a mortgage. Neither the public nor the private sector seems capable of addressing Speke's compound problems. Faced with this sustained failure, Mike and Doreen Knight, decided it was time they and other people did something about it for themselves.

It was Doreen who first got involved in the credit union, which was set up by the local vicar in 1989. By the mid-1990s the union was on the verge of collapse: the Knights took it by the scruff of the neck.

The credit union looks like a bank, the computerised tills are staffed by a team of 35 volunteers working on a rota. These are people like Yvonne Piroun and Sharon McGuffy. Yvonne is the single mother of three girls, the oldest of whom is twelve. By her own admission, she was going potty sitting at home all day until Doreen dragged her along to the credit union for a training course. Yvonne left school unable to read or write. Now she is the project's youth worker. Sharon, the single mother of four children, started as a volunteer and became the union's treasurer. The Knights have tapped into a seam of self-improvement and ambition among people on the estate that most top-down, state-sponsored schemes did not recognise.

Anyone on the estate can join the credit union, which is governed by a twelve-strong board of directors who are elected by the members. A member has to commit to save at least £67 over twelve months. If their savings record is good, they are eligible for a trial loan of £200, repayable over a year, at an interest rate of 1 per cent a month. Mike Knight estimates the credit union's APR is 12.7 per cent compared with 36 per cent through most hire purchase schemes, 45 per cent charged by mail order catalogues and 100 per cent charged by legal money lenders. The saver can then take out a second loan, of £500 or twice the amount they have saved with the union. When Doreen and Mike Knight took over the union the loan limit was £400; now its £1,000, a reflection of the higher level of saving the union has encouraged.

The union has already negotiated discounts for members booking holidays with local travel agents and purchasing white-goods from a local supplier. Mike Knight would like to be able to develop an enterprise fund to help local entrepreneurs set up their own businesses.

The union's ethic of mutual self-help does not mean it is soft. Far from it, Doreen Knight explained:

People come to us for a loan because they know we will listen to them sympathetically and understand their problems, because we come from round here. We will negotiate and re-negotiate their repayments for them in a way that the banks will not. But at the end of the day this is our members' money and we have to take responsibility for it. So if people start getting behind with their loans we have to have a way of dealing with it. We go to great lengths to find out why someone has stopped paying and what we can do to help. Often its because people have financial problems they are too embarrassed to talk about. But if none of that works we bring in debt collectors.

When the Knights took the helm, the credit union's 'delinquency' rate was 37 per cent; these days only 6 per cent of its loans are in serious arrears. Mike Knight's ambition is to create a credit union that brings together those who work and live in Speke, the employed and the unemployed, in mutual self-help.

Thousands of people work near Speke but don't live here. Take the Ford factory down the road. If we could get together with them to create a joint-credit union or even to administer a union on their behalf, we could become self-sustaining.

Leeds City Credit Union

Leeds City Credit Union is one of the most dynamic in the country. It has combined entrepreneurial management with strong membership involvement to build a thriving workplace based credit union, which is on the verge of expanding to bring in members from the surrounding community. Leeds City could thus become a model for a new hybrid credit union, which has a common bond that combines work and community.

When Sue Davenport took charge of the credit union in 1991, it had 800 members in the City Council and it took £120 a month in payroll deductions. By 1998 the Leeds City Credit Union, as it had become, had 7,000 members in 22 public sector organisations, nine staff, new offices and was collecting £650,000 a month through payroll deductions. The credit union's annual turnover is about £15 million, it has lent about £5 million and bad loans are just 0.7 per cent of its lending. Sue Davenport, who seems to have an instinctive grasp of how to combine a culture of entrepreneurship and co-operation, has ambitious plans to expand to 20,000 members by the end the year 2000. The credit union has taken over responsibility for credit union development from the council and is working with eleven other small, community-based credit unions in the city to share services with them.

Sue Davenport got involved in the credit union through her husband who was one of its founders in 1987. She started as a part-time helper but then in 1991 took over running the union. She explained the union's success:

Most community credit unions are set up because someone thinks they are a "good idea" for the community. But they have to be a professional business, offering competitive financial services. We have had to plan very carefully for growth; without business planning we could not have grown and without growth we could not have provided the services we do.

But the way we deliver is through our unique membership structure. Everything has to come from and go back to the members. This is not a faceless company. People understand it is their money and they want to look after it. We invest a huge amount in educating, informing and involving members and we pride ourselves on taking a professional but friendly and individual approach to people.

We have no lower limit on the amount people can borrow, so people can borrow as little as £150. The upper limit is £10,000. We charge very low interest rates on the loans – 1 per cent. Our return on savings is sometimes lower than those available through mainstream banks – 3 to 5 per cent – but it is far more stable because the rate of return is in the hands of the membership not the markets.

Leeds City's members are drawn from the council, universities, colleges of further education, the Citizens Advice Bureau and housing associations. The union is expanding into hospitals and recruiting members employed by private sector companies in Leeds city centre.

Birmingham Credit Union Development Agency

The Birmingham Credit Union Development Agency was set up in 1987 at the instigation of the city council's economic development department, which wanted to develop community credit unions in response to the closure of bank branches and growing evidence of financial exclusion among poorer communities in the city. The council believed credit unions might play an important role in economic regeneration and community development. The agency, which has a staff of seven, has developed into model for promoting not just individual credit unions but co-operation among clusters of credit unions so that they can make more of their combined strength. The agency is exploring opportunities for creating mutually advantageous joint ventures between groups of credit unions and banks.

Two-thirds of the population of Birmingham are covered by 30 credit unions: 27 community credit unions, with a membership of 5,500 and combined savings of about £2 million, and three workplace unions, with a membership of 10,000 and savings of about £8 million. The largest community credit unions have 1,000 members and a turnover of about £500,000 a year. The smallest have less than 100 members and a turnover of between £10,000 and £15,000. Women make up a majority of the members of credit unions and 66 per cent of the 380 the unions' volunteers. The agency has had public funding of at least £1 million over its twelve-year life.

The agency started its work by promoting the idea of credit unions and providing advice, support and training to people who wanted to found a union. However, its own research and learning has prompted it to expand its role. Jim Dearlove, the agency's co-ordinator explained:

> It's important we build on the foundations of what we have got. We think that is best done by encouraging clusters of credit unions to co-operate more. Most credit unions for example are open for one afternoon and one evening a week, often in a community centre or church hall. If we could get several small credit unions together they could jointly operate a high street shop in a large shopping centre, which could service all their members. It would also help to attract more new members. That could bring economies of scale which would allow the credit unions to expand and attract more members.

> It would be important to respect the social and local dimensions of credit unions. Our research shows that people value credit unions not just for the financial services, but because they are a place to meet, they can give volunteers access to skills they can use in applying for jobs and they give people a sense of contributing to their communities, that they are doing something useful. We have to maintain these social and community benefits while finding ways for credit unions to become financially stronger.

One problem facing some of the older, smaller community credit unions is that they were licensed to operate only in small areas, often a single housing estate. This meant they neither had a large enough nor affluent enough market to grow into. Some of the younger credit unions have been licensed to cover a larger area, with a mix of private and public housing. These newer credit unions are attempting to market themselves to people who already have bank and building society accounts, as well as people who have neither. Dearlove explained: 'You cannot help people out of financial exclusion if they are banded together in a credit union with other poor people. For a credit union to prosper, affluent and poor people have to be brought together.'

The agency's role in future may be to offer centralised services for credit unions to allow them to benefit from economies of scale, covering centralised banking, investment management, bill paying and marketing. This should allow credit unions to market a wider range of services and attract a larger membership.

The agency is exploring, with NatWest Bank, the possibility of the bank providing groups of credit unions with back office support and a range of financial products, for example mortgages, which credit unions cannot provide.

Future prospects
Established mutuals in financial services face mounting competitive pressures as a global process of consolidation creates larger, merged financial service providers, which should have economies of scale, lower costs and more to invest in building their brands. The capacity of mutuals to compete will depend on two factors.

First, they will need to defend their mutual status from attempts by members to convert to become a shareholder owned company. Legislation to make it harder for current members to profit from winding up a mutual would help this defence. Some mutuals feel as if they are conducting a continual election campaign to defend their mutual status.

Second, the mutuals will need to enhance the benefits of mutuality for their member-consumers. Price competitiveness is one aspect to this. The Nationwide, for example, stresses the way that mutual ownership allows it to have competitive interest rates because the society does not have to pay a dividend to shareholders. But in addition mutuals will have to find ways to involve, educate and inform members, for example using the Internet and telephone services, to create a stronger culture of membership and community roots, which should be vital to a mutual's brand image. Mutuals have to show that their membership structure promotes innovation that delivers higher quality and reinforces the membership culture.

The new mutuals, such as credit unions, offer the greatest potential for growth given that it is unlikely any new large building or friendly societies will be created. The scope for new community finance initiatives in the UK is suggested by the scale of credit union and community investment growth in the United States, the successful mutual guarantee societies and microfinance schemes in continental Europe, and community banking schemes in developing countries. The British community credit union movement in the UK is fragile and operates at the margins of mainstream financial provision.

Credit unions will only realise their potential with five main steps to strengthen their capacity.

First, community credit unions need clearer goals: the provision of first-class financial services in a community setting. Only if community credit unions provide a first-class service will they become centres for community regeneration.

Second, the movement needs to develop more professional paid managers rather than relying on hard-pressed volunteers. Models of best practice of managing in a mutual context need to be developed and disseminated.

Third, to provide that professional backing smaller community credit unions need a firmer institutional base. Many smaller credit unions might merge. One of the most promising possibilities is to create hybrid unions, which link workplace and community credit unions, along the lines of the Leeds City initiative. Another possibility would be for credit unions and banks to form joint ventures, in which banks provide management help and back-office functions for credit unions which undertake local marketing. Credit unions will only grow stronger by building bridges into mainstream financial services.

Fourth, the credit unions' capacity to grow will be eased by regulatory changes to allow them to offer a wider range of products, including mortgages.

Fifth, a federated mutual movement like community credit unions is strongest at a local level. One of their weaknesses is their lack of strategic management to set new targets, build new capabilities, adjust to new circumstances and reap economies of scale. The Birmingham Credit Union Development Agency is one model for how that can be achieved at a local level. Strong national bodies are also essential to spread best practice. The British credit union movement suffers from the fragmentation of its national leadership. The UK should develop a national organisation to service credit unions, modeled on the Credit Union Services Corporation in Australia. This is a promising model of how to combine local self help and know-how with a national strategy.

3.8 Employment
History and extent
Mutuals have long helped to organise the supply of labour, from guilds through to modern trade unions and professional associations. Trade unions are among the largest and for some the most controversial mutual organisations. They played a critical role in the development of other mutuals, such as the co-operative movement.

Trade union membership has been in decline since the late 1970s. There were 12 million union members in 1979. In 1997 membership was down to 6.8 million, about 30 per cent of the employed workforce, compared with 39 per cent in 1989. Recently the TUC announced a modest increase in membership to about 7 million, the first for many years. The decline of unions is primarily a product of structural changes that shifted work from manufacturing to services, large companies to small, full-time to part-time jobs and men to women. Unions were slow to respond to these shifts. Even in periods of employment growth such as 1986–89 when the number of employees in employment went up by 1.4 million, union membership declined, by 5.5 per cent in 1989 alone. In addition, legislation in the 1980s and 1990s undermined trade union's bargaining power.

Alongside trade unions, some of which are trying to modernise their services and extend their appeal, there are emerging examples of new mutuals that are seeking co-operative solutions to problems of unemployment, skills mismatch or insecurity. For example, in the UK there are about 150 telecottages, resources centres for home-based teleworkers, mainly in rural areas. About 40 telecottages in Wales service some 2,000 teleworkers.

There are about 270 Local Exchange and Trading Schemes (LETS) in the UK. In a LETS people trade with one another using a special currency to encourage the use of local services, thus strengthening the local economy. The initial findings from a recent unpublished survey, conducted in 1998 by Queen Mary and Westfield College London in conjunction with Leicester University, has found about 270 active LETS, with a combined membership of perhaps 19,450 and an annual turnover of £1.2 millions. The oldest and best established schemes, for example Stroud in Gloucestershire, involve businesses as well as individuals. The largest schemes, for example in north London, have around 300 members.

Strengths and weaknesses
Trade unions. Unions are still strong among large employers – 85 of the companies listed in the FTSE 100 are unionised – and in the public sector, where about 70 per cent of the workforce are union members. The unions have weathered a storm of change and hostile legislation: the worst may be over. Unionised employers have not embarked on large-scale de-unionisation drives. Trade union organisation has been strengthened through mergers. Some unions show signs of renewal by introducing new services, such as the Unison plan to create a pension scheme for low-income members, a GMB plan to create a regionally based credit union and the Iron and Steel Trade Confederation initiative to promote 'community based unionism'.

However, structural trends in the labour market are still running against the unions, which are poorly organised in the fastest growing parts of the economy: small companies, service sectors and among women and young people. Only 20 per cent of under 25-year-olds are union members. Union membership is only 11 per cent among hotel workers and 17 per cent in retailing. New initiatives to improve recruitment and retention have been talked about since the mid-1980s but few have born fruit. Union officials have strong incentives to serve current members rather than invest in recruiting new members. As a result unions are constantly prey to the conservatism that can infect older mutuals.

New mutuals. The new mutuals – telecottages, self-help groups, mentoring initiatives – are aimed at a growing need: providing greater security for people working in flexible, insecure labour markets. They might build upon the success of job club and mentoring initiatives to engage the unemployed in collaborative self-help finding jobs and could use new technologies. However, it is difficult to get self-help initiatives started without some full-time support or the support of a larger institution. Employee mutuals, based in the community, may find it hard to establish a clear, common bond. People do not want 'second best' self-help schemes, which are regarded as a 'poor man's' version of the market. This is one reason why consumers are unwilling to join LETS.

Case studies
The employee mutual

A detailed plan for an Employee Mutual was set out in a Demos pamphlet published last year: *The Employee Mutual: Combining flexibility and security in the new world of work.*[39]

The employee mutual would be an intermediary that helped people to find work, employers to fill vacancies, and workers and businesses, especially small companies, to meet shared needs for training and childcare. The mutual would be like a club, the members of which would help one another cope with the turbulence of the modern labour market. Its job would be to solve problems faced by small employers in particular, as well as serving the unemployed, the self-employed and those in work.

The mutual would be run by a small full-time team that would organise members to provide one another with self-help. For example a job-search co-ordinator would help to train and organise job hit-squads which would scour the locality for work on behalf of mutual members. A benefits adviser would train members to help one another with their claims. A childcare co-ordinator would help members get together to run a nursery, crèche facilities and childcare at home.

A member would join the employee mutual by signing a covenant that would commit him or her to help other members of the mutual and to contribute to the mutual's resources, either financially or through services in kind. In return, members would be entitled to use services provided by the employee mutual, such as training courses. Members would earn points on a 'club card' which would show what services they could 'buy' from the mutual. This employee mutual idea could be applied in several different settings.

- A project funded by Birmingham City Council – Sustainable Strength – is attempting to create a network among self-employed Asian women.
- Self-employed fashion designers and musicians often work within informal networks of collaboration, often developed around a college, such as Goldsmiths in south London, to which they return to teach or for further study. These networks around colleges and universities could provide a base for a mutual.
- Mutuals could develop from mentoring schemes designed to help people through the transition into work. In one group mentoring programme run by Employment Links in Liverpool, about 50 long-term unemployed people over the age of 50 have counselled and supported one another through the process of training and job search. About fifteen got jobs within six months of the programme starting, a far higher success rate than other schemes for this age group.

Wise Group Mutual

The idea of an employee mutual is being taken forward by the Wise Group in Glasgow, which has developed effective and innovative schemes to get the long-term unemployed back into work. Construction and home-improvement companies set up by the Wise Group have created at least 250 jobs. The group runs training and work experience courses for about 1,500 people a year. Last year 55 per cent of the 1,100 people who entered its most demanding work experience programmes got jobs. About 90 per cent of trainees who complete Wise Group programmes get jobs. The group recently created its own telephone call centre to give long-term unemployed people work experience they need to get a call centre job. The Wise Group has ambitious plans to expand to 5,000 trainees within four years.

The group plans to combine this expansion with an employee mutual which all trainees would be eligible to join. They would remain members once they had left one of the training schemes. The aim of the mutual is set out as 'providing a sophisticated, cohesive and structured package of support to people when they leave our programmes which will help them find and retain jobs and access further education.' The mutual would keep in contact with trainees, provide access to financial services such as debt counselling and credit union savings schemes, help organise co-operative childcare and provide access to continuous learning opportunities as well as information about job vacancies. The mutual would be run by a small central team, which would co-ordinate the efforts of scores of unpaid local agents on housing estates around Glasgow.

Training Pounds

Training Pounds is a scheme developed by the New Economics Foundation for SoLo, the Training and Enterprise Council in south London. The scheme is modelled on WIV, the Swiss scheme worth SWFr1 billion a year, in which companies trade within one another for services in kind using a special currency.

The Training Pounds scheme would create a special currency that could only be used by members and spent on training. The aim is to use spare capacity on in-house company training schemes to satisfy unmet demand for training among job seekers. Someone who wanted training would join the scheme and incur a debt in training pounds by taking a spare place on a training programme run by a company. A basic course in Windows 98 might cost ten training pounds. A trainee could pay-off this ten training pounds debt by training other people in the skills they had learned. A company that made available a place for training this person would earn ten training pounds which it could then spend training its own employees on courses provided by other companies in the scheme.

Unison Stakeholder Pension Plan

The Unison stakeholder pension plan is a good example of traditional mutuals working together to create a new service. Unison has developed a detailed plan for a 'stakeholder' pension that is designed to serve the needs to 4 million low-paid workers, many earning less than £100 per week, who do not have a second pension. The plan was developed with the help of the Liverpool Victoria Friendly Society, the Britannia Building Society and a firm of actuaries.

Unison wants to create a pension scheme for people who do not have access to an employer scheme and who do not wish to join a private pension plan. The Unison stakeholder pension plan would pay defined benefits for contributors. The funds would be managed by a set of six or seven mutuals, thereby creating room for comparison of performance and competition. The employer and employee would contribute to the scheme with contributions rising as an employee ages.

Unison's assistant general secretary Roger Poole believes the union's expertise in representing low-paid workers would enable it to recruit hundreds of thousands of employees into the scheme. An established mutual, the union, would be the gateway for people to join a new mutual pension scheme, which would be administered by established mutuals in the financial services sector.

Future prospects
Trade unions, which have weathered two decades of disruption and decline, may have stabilised. There are signs of renewal and innovation, although much of this innovation has yet to make an impact on how trade unions are regarded by the public. The prospects for mutuality in employment largely depend on how imaginative and entrepreneurial unions can become in developing a wider role, which would include services such as lifelong learning and pension planning.

There seems to be a clear need for new 'employee mutuals', which could provide people with greater security within a more flexible, uncertain labour market. Neither the state nor the market seems well placed to meet the needs for training, job search and childcare, especially among the self-employed, small businesses, younger workers and those on low incomes. However establishing and growing such mutuals will take time, money and learning.

3.9 Mutuality in business
History and extent
Agriculture. There were 544 farmer-controlled businesses in 1997, down from 636 in 1984, of which 531 were co-operatives and thirteen were other forms of joint operation. These businesses had a turnover of £7.4

billion and 243,000 farmer members, according to the Plunkett Foundation. About 131,000 farmers were members of co-operatives or jointly owned businesses supplying farm equipment and material; 104,000 were members of co-operatives that marketed produce and 18,000 were members of co-operatives supplying other farm related services. At that time there were 281,000 farmers in the UK, 166,000 full-time and 114,000 part-time. Co-operatives employed 13,300 people in 1997, down from 16,000 in 1984.

Co-operatives had a monopoly in marketing wool and the Milk Marque had 85 per cent of the British milk market, handling 7 billion litres of milk a year, provided by 18,000 dairy farmer co-operative members. Marketing co-operatives accounted for 95 per cent of British apples, 74 per cent of cauliflower, 63 per cent of raspberries, 60 per cent of lettuces, 57 per cent of peas and 50 per cent of pears, 37 per cent of the oil seed market, 35 per cent of potatoes, 32 per cent of eggs and 34 per cent of pigs.

Retail and consumer co-operatives. The British co-operative movement claims 9 million members. The co-operative is still a leading retailer, albeit far smaller than it used to be. At the end of 1997 co-operative retailers had 6 per cent of the grocery market, worth about £5.2 billion. Cooperative retailing was more significant in the grocery trade than Morrisons, Waitrose, Iceland or Marks & Spencer. Retail co-operatives as a whole employ about 120,000 people, with revenues of about £8.5 billion.

The co-operative movement's loss of market share has been pronounced. Between the late 1950s and the mid-1990s, the co-op share of the UK retailing market as a while fell from 11 per cent to close to 4 per cent. At its peak in the 1950s there were 900-plus co-operative societies in the UK, with almost 30,000 shops; in 1998 there were just 46 societies, with 4,600 shops. However retail co-ops have expanded in some areas. The Co-op's share of the holiday market has gone from close to zero to about 10 per cent over the past two decades and The Co-op provides one in four British funerals.

Employee owned businesses and worker co-operatives. Employee share ownership is quite widespread in the UK, through save as you earn schemes. However employee ownership of companies, through an Employee Share Ownership Plan (ESOP), is relatively rare. Capital Strategies, the corporate finance house that specialises in employee ownership plans, estimates 670 companies operate an Employee Share Ownership Plan that covers most employees of the company. Most of these schemes are a financial vehicle for companies quoted on the stock exchange to provide shares for employees in a tax efficient way. The number of ESOPs through which employees control a significant stake in their company is much lower. There are some outstanding examples of innovative employee ownership companies, such as St Luke's, the advertising agency, and FI Group, the software company. However there are perhaps only 50 of these schemes among private companies. This contrasts with the United States where the National Centre for Employee Ownership estimates there are 8,500 employee ownership companies, with perhaps 800,000 employees, that operate an ESOP, providing share options for all employees or employee owner-ship investment plans, known as 401K plans.

There are about 1,500 worker co-operatives in the UK, employing about 15,000 people. Although there are outstanding success stories, such as the Tower Colliery in South Wales, Tayside Buses and Greenwich Leisure, the worker co-operative movement in the UK is very small compared to Spain, Italy and some other parts of continen-tal Europe.

Electronic mutuals. The ethic of mutuality plays an important role in emerging models of business organisation, designed to allow compa-nies to mobilise the know-how and commitment of employees, suppli-ers, partners and consumers. The idea that companies should use the Internet to build electronic consumer communities around a brand was a central feature of *Net Gain: Expanding markets through virtual communities* by John Hagel III and Arthur G Armstrong.[40] Hagel and Armstrong argue that companies that pursue this strategy will have to be much more open with their consumers, share more information and be more accountable.

The power of this new approach is its ability to blur the line between producers and consumers, by enlisting consumers as joint producers, designers and innovators of products and services. The best example of the potential for this new mutual approach is the growth of the Linux operating system profiled below. Electronic commerce may also provide the basis for global co-operation, particularly in financial markets. Some of the world's biggest insurance companies and brokers are planning to create a co-operative, global e-commerce trading network to link Rinet, the Brussels-based organisation that links continental European reinsurers, Win, the global organisation owned by the world's four largest insurance brokers, and Limnet, which links up the London insurance market. The stated aim of this electronic co-operative is to respond to a squeeze on profit margins by cutting administration costs.

Strengths and weaknesses
Consumer mutuals. The main strength of consumer mutuals is their ability to create a sense of membership commitment and loyalty. The best co-operatives – see the profile of the Oxford, Swindon and Gloucester Co-operative below – use their membership structure to unlock innovation and new ideas. Co-operatives do not have to make a return for shareholders, which should give them greater leeway to adopt socially responsible approaches to business. Co-operatives have not opened many out-of-town shopping centres and instead have focused on smaller convenience shops, often in villages and poorer urban centres.

However, co-operative retailers delayed innovating in the face of intense competition, in part because their ownership structure cushioned them from financial pressures. They underestimated their traditional strengths, such as the 'consumer dividend', failed to include members in a meaningful way and did not deliver high enough standards of quality of service.

Producer mutuals. These may become more common as a defensive response to more competitive and open markets, for example as subsidies are withdrawn and tariffs reduced in agricultural markets. The electronic co-operative planned for the insurance industry fits into this category.

Producer co-operatives can be quite robust as long as they organise producers of a fairly homogenous commodity product; competition between producers based on innovation and quality is limited and there is a simple way to calculate how much members should put in and take out of the co-operative. All these features are present in the British wool and milk industries, which is one reason co-operatives accounts for such a large share of production in these industries.

Producer co-operatives are far less effective in markets with high rates of innovation and in industries where producers compete on quality and service as well as price. In faster moving, more open and innovative industries it is far more difficult to organise and maintain agreement among producers.

Employee owned business. It should become more common for employees to have a stake in the business they work for. The appeal of employee ownership is their capacity to unlock the ideas, tacit know-how and imagination of employees, who stand to gain from the wealth they help to create through employee ownership. Employee ownership and stock-option plans have become common in the United States in high-growth, knowledge-intensive businesses such as software, Internet services and biotechnology, which depend heavily on employee involvement and know-how. The downside is that employee owned businesses, and worker co-operatives in particular, can become conservative, inward looking and slow to innovate. Co-operatives, quite rationally, tend to prioritise the needs of current members, over those of future or potential members. As a result they are often organised to protect the interests of 'insiders' who may have a limited appetite for change and growth. Co-operatives tend to have egalitarian pay structures, designed to avoid conflict, dissent and division. This provides little reward or incentive for innovation.

Electronic mutuals. Mutual business models are well placed to exploit the potential of Internet or Web technologies to bring together dispersed, independent producers and consumers. In the past, co-ordination of many independent producers and consumers would have been possible only through markets or large corporations. Electronic networks may allow closer co-ordination of otherwise independent actors. The strength of these new electronic mutuals is this capacity to combine independence and co-ordination and to blur the line between consumption and production.

Some business theorists argue that electronic mutuals are the shape of the organisation of the future.[41] However they also have significant weaknesses. Electronic consumer clubs, such as Linux, thrive on the enthusiasm of specialists and computer buffs. They may prove too time consuming, particularly for general consumers. Electronic mutuals may be good at orchestrating incremental improvements to a product, but they are less adept at the kind of radical innovation and knowledge creation needed to get a product off the ground in the first place. This radical innovation may be too difficult for dispersed networks. The Linux club, for example, started with Linus Torvalds, an entrepreneur, taking the risk of putting his fledging operating system onto the Internet.

Case studies
Linux : the electronic mutual

In October 1991, Linus Torvalds, a 21-year-old computer science student at Helsinki University, posted on the Internet the kernel of a rudimentary computer operating system called Linux: a basic version of the Unix operating system widely used in companies and large computer networks. Torvalds invited other programmers to download his creation, tinker with it and improve it. Gradually people took up Torvalds' offer and as the Linux club membership went into the thousands, the fledgling operating system started to attract more attention. In the past two years Linux has gone from a specialist product, designed for buffs, by buffs, into a robust, efficient, freely distributed but widely used global product. The system has won endorsements from IBM, Intel, Oracle, Sun Microsystems, Hewlett-Packard, Silicon Graphics, Compaq and Dell. In 1998 the number of companies using Linux went up by 30 per cent. Two years ago Linux had 1.5 million members; now it runs on about 10 million computers including systems at Nasa, Boeing, Wells Fargo Bank and the US Postal Service.

Torvalds attributes Linux's success to the organisation that created it. Linux is 'open source software' developed in a collaborative effort, by enthusiasts inspired by the idea that software should be fast, reliable, functional and free. Advocates of open source software insist products made this way are better than traditional commercial software because they are tested over and over by members of the electronic mutual: global, electronic peer review. Glitches are hard to hide. Consumers are not confused by marketing hype. Torvalds described the project this way:

> *It's supposed to be good technically but fun as well. There's also the social side to it, of having a lot of people around I really enjoy working with. And then there is the gratification, the knowledge that you are doing something that people consider important. It makes you feel meaningful.*

Thomas W Malone and Robert J Laubacher from the Sloan School of Management at the Massachusetts Institute of Technology are leading a research programme to discern the emerging shape of organisations in the twenty-first century. They put Linux's organisational strengths this way:

> *The Linux story really shows us the power of new technology – in this case, electronic networks – to fundamentally change the way that work is done. The Linux community, a temporary, self-managed gathering of diverse individuals engaged in a common task, is a model for a new kind of business organisation that could form the basis for a new kind of economy.*

The Linux business model has four distinctive advantages. First, it is highly creative. The communal self-help ethos has helped to unlock the ideas of enthusiasts around the world, ideas that they would not have given to a profit-making company. The open-access, electronic network has created a transparent system of peer review, through which ideas can be proposed, tested and justified. Second, enthusiasts are prepared to contribute their ideas because they are attached to the project's sense of purpose: to create free, functional software which trades on its utility not its brand image. The electronic mutual can be trusted. Third, as a result the Linux mutual has tremendous cost advantages. The enthusiast members have made their knowledge freely available and the software is distributed over the Internet, virtually free. The marketing is done 'virally' by word of mouth among users. The brand image of Linux – free, efficient, functional, trustworthy – has been built up incrementally and without an expensive advertising campaign. Using these cost advantages Linux was able to start small in markets overlooked by larger players among specialists but then migrate up-market into more established higher-value markets in larger corporations.[42] The very low-cost structure of the Linux system has made it a radical commercial insurgent not just a technical innovator. Fourth, the mutual 'ownership' structure of Linux – it isn't owned by anyone although Linus Torvalds is in effect its technical director – means that Microsoft cannot buy it up, as it has done with other promising challengers to its position.

CMG Group: new model for employee ownership

CMG is just one of a new breed of innovative, employee owned companies in knowledge intensive industries, in this case, software. Cornelius Stutterheim, the chairman of CMG, the fast growing computer services group, sums up his corporate philosophy thus:

> We have to realise and then act upon the realisation that our most important asset is our most mobile asset and it is not recorded on our balance sheet: it's our people. This asset fills up every morning and waters down each evening. The awareness of that means you have to treat people in the way that you would like to be treated yourself.

CMG was created in 1964 by three founders who were fed up with the stuffy bureaucracy of the large companies they then worked for. It styled itself as a progressive but paternalistic company. CMG promoted an open culture of reward according to merit, but most of its shares was held by the founders until the mid-1980s. When the founders decided to sell their stakes the current management team took the opportunity to create a broadly based employee ownership culture through an employee buy-out. Employee ownership is combined with a free flow of information and open decision making.

There are no executive offices at CMG and everyone has the same kind of desk. The company is open with information to the extent that any employee can look at any other employee's personnel file, including information about their salary and bonuses. If someone wants to challenge another employee's salary, executives are obliged to respond to the query. Stutterheim believes an open flow of information is vital to create an environment in which people take responsibility for their actions with minimal interference from executives.

As well as being open, the company prides itself on being entrepreneurial and meritocratic. Pay is set by an annual open review of employee performance. Managers are demoted as well as promoted. CMG keeps work units small. No unit is allowed to grow beyond 80 people; if it does, it must be split into smaller units.

In October 1995 when the company was listed on the stock market, about 1,000 directors and employees and about 850 ex-employees and their relatives, together with employee trusts and pension schemes, owned about 90 per cent of the company. The shareholding of current employees has been reduced to about 30 per cent.

The top 70 executives are required to own CMG shares worth a year's salary. The next 170 managers are required to hold shares worth six month's salary. The company runs a share option scheme, which is funded by payroll deductions and open to all employees. This share option scheme is extremely popular. In the last offering almost 60 per cent of employees elected to take part.

Innovation in a traditional retail co-operative

In the early 1990s the Oxford, Swindon and Gloucester co-operatives were mired in financial trouble. In the 1970s the separate co-operative societies that now make up the combined group suffered from many of the drawbacks of traditional co-operatives. They had become introspective and slow-moving. The board did not challenge the management, the management had lost its focus on the consumer and competition, and members were not actively involved in the society. After considerable management upheaval, following the merger of the societies in 1991, the new management set out to modernise the society by improving both its business performance and its membership involvement.

The society has invested in its 72 main convenience and food stores, built up its image as a retailer that specialises in inner-city and community shops, and expanded its activities in car dealerships, funerals and travel. The quality of its stores has improved and it has recruited new staff from commercial retailers.

The society has also set out to actively manage and engage its membership base. As Peter Couchman, its membership and marketing manager explained: 'We have to use our ownership structure to unlock innovation and that means we have to go back to the membership.' The first task was to get an accurate grasp of the size and make-up of the membership base. Nominally Oxford, Swindon and Gloucester had 150,000 members, but in reality the active membership was closer to 20,000. The membership was far older than the customer base. The society has engaged members by holding regular, small, informal meetings and it has plans to use the telephone and the Internet to widen these informal channels of communication. Staff are being trained to communicate with customers as members. The society is also communicating the values of membership more aggressively. Oxford, Swindon and Gloucester devotes 1 per cent of its profits to other co-ops and a further 1 per cent to community projects, a far higher proportion of profits than most quoted companies.

Peter Couchman put the society's goals this way:

We are trying to adapt nineteenth century structures to compete in the twenty-first century as a successful co-operative business. The nineteenth century structures are rigid and linear; we are creating a more organic way for people to have a sense of involvement.

As yet the financial results are impressive. In the past five years, sales have risen by 27 per cent and trading profit by 60 per cent.

Future prospects
Mutuals in commercial fields are engaged in a constant battle against becoming too inward looking and too concerned with the needs of their current members. These are tendencies that lead mutuals towards conservatism and complacency.

Some producer mutuals are set up to defend their members. Producer co-operatives of the kind which abound in agriculture may become more common in industries that provide commodity products to an intensely competitive market.

In most business sectors, mutuals will thrive only by making the most of their distinctive strengths based on their sense of membership to innovate new products and services in open, competitive markets. The best mutuals – Linux is an outstanding example – have a compelling sense of purpose that engages their membership in improving a product which can compete with the best offered by a commercial company. Such mutuals have an engaged membership and dynamic management, set high standards for quality and are open to competition and ideas from the outside. Managing this mix is very demanding but offers large rewards.

There is considerable scope to expand employee ownership and all-employee stock option plans in the UK, especially among young, privately owned companies in knowledge intensive fields such as software and multimedia. In the US employee share ownership plans have grown mainly among smaller, privately quoted companies in which the founders have sold out to their employees. This is uncommon in the UK: there are ESOPs in only 35 private companies. Capital Strategies estimates there could be scope for at least 500.

The prospects for consumer mutuals, such as the co-operative retailers, depends on whether they can deploy their ownership structure to unlock more innovation and loyalty than commercial retailers. Co-operatives should be able to use electronic networks to do this. Consumer co-operatives may also be able to exploit their reputation for trust and social responsibility, particularly in informing consumers about risks to do with food. A consumer co-operative is accountable to members, not shareholders; thus it should have no incentive to mislead consumers, for instance over the risks associated with genetically modified food.

In addition there could be considerable scope for the creation of new consumer mutuals to organise blocks of consumers in the liberalised markets for gas and electricity, combining their buying power to exploit economies of scale. One organisation – EquiGas – is already marketing a mutual approach to gas buying.

Electronic mutuals, born from collaborative activity on the Internet, have great potential. New kinds of consumer mutuals and clubs might emerge. For example, Internet auctions might develop into mutuals or clubs through which independent producers buy and sell their services. Wingham Rowan has proposed the creation of guaranteed electronic markets, which would allow local producers to trade with one another electronically through a market they would sign up to join, just as finance houses are members of the stockexchange.[43] The growth of Linux shows that electronic networks can co-ordinate dispersed independent producers and consumers very effectively.

3.10 Environment
History and extent
Mutuality has long been associated with environmental concerns. In the late nineteenth century, mutualism was linked to initiatives to provide better public health for town dwellers, protect the country-side, develop allotments and create new settlements – notably the Garden City movement of the early twentieth century. This strain of mutualism has been pushed to the margins. Town and country planning, environmental protection and management of local amenities have become dominated by 'top-down' developments regulated by local and national government and often delivered by the private sector. Yet mutualist culture is a powerful presence in the Green movement and it could become much more important.

Environmentalist thought emphasises the need to safeguard the shared environmental 'commons' – clean air, water, soil, fisheries, forests – because unregulated market activity in these areas can lead to unsustainable consumption and degradation of resources. Mutual recognition of rights and responsibilities in using the environmental commons is a key principle of the new politics of the environment.[44]

Concern over environmental degradation became a matter of widespread concern in the 1970s. Since then membership of conservation and environmentalist campaigns has grown enormously. From the National Trust and the RSPB, to Friends of the Earth and Greenpeace, environmental groups in the non-profit sector have tapped huge reservoirs of support for protection of the environment, landscapes, wildlife and amenities such as parks. Many environmental groups espouse a mutualist philosophy of shared responsibility, which often chimes with other mutual initiatives, for example in community-led economic development. This could open up scope for collaboration between community development mutuals and environmental campaigns to create environment mutuals.

This development is making itself felt in the emerging 'social economy'. Many LETS schemes are rooted in a desire to create a socially and environmentally sustainable local economy. Organic food-box schemes with an environmentalist ethos serve more than 35,000 members, and organic food co-ops can provide a way of combining the agendas of sustainable development and social inclusion, offering fresh food services to low-income communities. There are more than 500 community recycling schemes and community composting schemes, and some 2500 community transport schemes. Business environment clubs, established often in partnership between the private sector, local authorities and non-profit bodies offer advice and information on environmental regulations, technologies and market opportunities, especially for small and medium-sized enterprises.

Every local authority is required to draw up by 2000 an action plan under the umbrella of Local Agenda 21 (LA21), an initiative that promotes local strategies for environmentally sustainable and socially responsible economic development, often based on community consultations. The official drive to have LA21 plans in every local authority area gives considerable scope for the development of mutualist approaches to local planning. LA21 has been instrumental in promoting mutual developments: partnerships between business, local government and voluntary groups; new forms of community consultation to build up a shared local vision of how an area should develop; and 'community-owned' indicators of local quality of life and progress to sustainable development.

Strengths and weaknesses
A sense of mutual responsibility is central to environmentalism, which is one of the most powerful social movements of the last generation and likely to be one of the main growth sectors in the social economy. The key source of strength behind mutualism in relation to the environment is the growing convergence between the environmentalist policy agenda and those of social inclusion and community regeneration.

Good examples of the potentially powerful convergence of non-profit organisations that aim to link environmental sustainability and social fairness are the Groundwork movement and Neighbourhood

Energy Action. Neither are formal mutuals but they frequently help the development of collaborative self-help at a community level.

Environmentally sustainable approaches will require organisational innovations that rely on local commitment and know-how. Mutuals are well suited to garnering this commitment, which is often beyond the scope of the public or private sectors. In transport, for example, the key need is for more flexible, user friendly forms of public transport. In recycling, we need approaches to waste collection and recycling that can generate local jobs and wealth as well as reduce waste. The community sector – non-profit community-based enterprises, which share a mutualist ethos if not a mutual structure – has been vital in building up domestic waste recycling schemes.[45] Householders are more motivated to take part in schemes run by community bodies than those run by private firms or local authorities. In some sectors (such as composting) there are diseconomies of scale: production and consumption are more effective when organised through the informal economy or through micro enterprises closely linked to a community. Mutual solutions, geared to achieving social and environmental outcomes through innovative enterprises, could make sustainable solutions viable.

Alongside these strengths the mutual approach suffers several shortcomings:

- The links between environmental and social agendas are underdeveloped in the work of many environmental groups.
- The regulatory and market frameworks do not yet give powerful enough incentives for the development of mutual approaches to energy saving, public transport, car sharing, food and community recycling.
- LA21 has made patchy progress: in many areas it is seen as a marginal concern and less important in economic development than inward investment or other familiar approaches.

But despite these weaknesses, the potential for mutual approaches in environmental improvement is high, as shown in the two case studies below.

Case studies
Ealing Community Transport
'Where there's muck, there's brass' is an old saw which might gain a new lease of life as mutuals develop the community recycling marketplace. Ealing Community Transport started life as a small community group providing public transport with a turnover of £60,000 in 1985. Waste recycling has helped it to diversify into an environmental enterprise, turning over some £6 million and employing 180 staff in 1998.

Groundwork: sustainable regeneration for communities

The Groundwork movement, set up in 1981, is one of the UK's leading environmental regeneration bodies. Groundwork, a non-profit organisation funded by government, business, local authorities and charitable foundations, is a federal network of over 40 autonomous local trusts in England, Wales and Ulster that design and deliver local projects for environmental improvement in partnership with community groups, business and local government. Groundwork focuses especially on urban areas and urban fringes and increasingly seeks to link its work on improving local environments with the development of new jobs, skills, educational schemes and businesses in disadvantaged communities. Groundwork runs many projects with its partners, ranging from urban forestry schemes to programmes such as Youth Works for preventing at-risk young people entering crime (see case study in section 3.6 above) to initiatives for environmental education. In many cases, Groundwork Trusts act as facilitators of mutual initiatives, as when they develop projects with tenants' associations, LETS, Green business clubs and community forums. A powerful example of Groundwork's approach to local partnerships is the regeneration of the Wren's Nest Estate in the Black Country. Groundwork and many other bodies have collaborated in gaining resources for environmental improvements for this deprived estate that have not only enhanced the physical environment but also led to new training programmes, community facilities and job creation. The Wren's Nest Estate projects are developed in partnership with the tenants' association and community centre, promoting a co-operative ethos and placing major emphasis on the involvement of residents in designing and implementing projects and making decisions about the future of the estate.

Recycling accounts for 80 per cent ECT's turnover. One in eight Londoners has access to ECT's kerbside collection service for household waste. ECT is an increasingly serious competitor for local authority household waste recycling contracts and is probably the biggest single enterprise in the community recycling sector.

The organisation is a non-profit member-owned charity: ECT is a mutualist group comprising ECT Recycling, ECT Engineering and Lambeth Community Recycling. Andy Bond, ECT Recycling's managing

---

Neighbourhood energy action: energy saving and projects to combact fuel poverty

Neighbourhood Energy Action (NEA) is a charity that aims to combat the serious problem of fuel poverty among many low-income households – in particular by promoting measures to save energy. By focusing on home insulation and other energy conservation and efficiency measures for low-income households and communities, NEA aims to achieve both environmental and social policy goals. Its activities – typically pursued in partnership with organisations in the public, private and voluntary sectors – include provision of energy saving advice and information, energy efficiency awareness campaigns and promotion of clubs for fuel savers. Better insulation reduces fuel bills for people on low budgets and also brings environmental benefits. Like the WISE Group in Scotland, NEA also seeks to create jobs in energy saving – for example, through insulation provision – for people in areas of high unemployment. NEA is not itself a mutual, but like Groundwork it helps to promote mutual associations and projects that have a mutualist dimension. NEA often works with partners such as tenants' associations, credit unions and other mutual aid bodies to promote energy saving and reduce fuel poverty. Initiatives include the setting up of mutual schemes such as fuel co-ops for low-income householders: the fuel co-op or fuel savers' club is a means of preventing fuel poverty by negotiating energy tariffs on behalf of all members, providing independent information, advice and training for householders, and assisting with metering and bill payment to prevent people falling into hardship or self-disconnecting from utilities. NEA and its partners have helped set up mutual aid groups such as fuel savers' clubs with tenants' associations and community self-help groups in many areas where the risk of fuel poverty is high.

director, describes the group as a highly flexible structure to which mutual status is 'crucial – it attracted the people we have in the first place, and they've been critical to our success'. The mutualist ethos helps to attract innovative and committed staff drawn to ECT by environmentalist and community spirit. But Andy Bond believes mutualism makes ECT attractive to many local authorities and to the public. ECT is an entrepreneurial mutual: it has developed new approaches to recycling by engaging its customers – for example, tenants' associations – in discussions to work out jointly the best waste collection methods. ECT works only by making waste collection a mutual activity with customers.

ECT's approach has many strengths, but Andy Bond is aware of the strains brought by success, which has attracted growing competition from the private sector. ECT wants to grow but this will challenge its mutual culture, not least because the group will need to develop still more its professional management skills. Managing these stresses is a challenge to a growing mutual which needs to become still more professional in operation while retaining the open culture and co-operative ethic that provide its competitive edge.

Andy Bond is confident that ECT can continue to combine innovation and growth with a mutualist ethos of open communication and partnership with staff and clients. However ECT's task would be helped if finance for growth were easier to find for organisations with novel corporate structures. Bond argues the Best Value framework for purchasing by local authorities needs to provide a level playing field for the community sector. So far, however, ECT has maintained its lead, demonstrating how a mutual enterprise culture can generate innovation and growth in the new economy of environmentally sustainable development.

CADISPA

Remote rural communities survive only with a spirit of mutual aid and co-operative working. Conservation and Development in Sparsely Populated Areas (CADISPA) is an experimental initiative in sustainable development that aims to help rural communities reconcile local economic development with conservation and protection of the environment. CADISPA is a family of research and development projects across Europe, run from its university base in Glasgow, which works in partnership with small and remote communities on environmental education, community-based decision-making and facilitation of community bids for resources that will promote local development that is environmentally and socially sustainable. A mutualist ethic is central to the programme, whose Director Geoff Fagan says that mutuality 'makes absolute sense as the way to build sustainable communities'.

CADISPA began in 1988 as a collaboration between the Green charity World Wildlife Fund UK and the Jordanhill College of Education, now part of the University of Strathclyde in Glasgow. The project expanded to take in work in Italy, Spain and Portugal and, after the Rio Earth Summit of 1992, it was given support by the European Union to develop environmental education for small 'peripheral' communities. CADISPA is the main programme within the university's new Centre for Sustainable Community Development.

CADISPA facilitates new thinking by remote communities on how they can improve their quality of life and integrate economic development with environmental well-being. On the Scottish island of Tiree, for example, CADISPA worked with local groups to help them gain more control over planning for local development. It was instrumental in helping citizens form community groups that articulated a common agenda for improving local facilities and prepared bids for funding from the EU and the Scottish Office. Empowering local people means challenging established forms of ownership and service delivery: for example, on Tiree, the community wants the new community centre to be run as a co-operative, not by the local authority. Helping community groups and public officials work out a new mutualist approach to sustainable local development means helping to change cultures and expectations on both sides, a time-consuming and error-prone process. CADISPA promotes 'mutual learning by doing' in rural community development. Its lessons are likely to be relevant to people in many urban areas as well as those in remote rural communities.[46]

Future prospects
The rise of environmental policy concerns, the advent of LA21 and the commitment at all levels of government and business to sustainable development all suggest environmental concerns and community

development will increasingly converge around sustainable development. There will be considerable scope for further development of groups such as Groundwork and NEA, which foster community organisations with environmental, social and economic goals. There are clear opportunities for mutuals to grow in community recycling and transport, as shown by ECT, and for facilitators of local mutualism such as the CADISPA project.

Environmental mutuals need a more supportive framework. Perhaps most importantly the Best Value framework for tendering for local authority contracts could be redesigned to promote a mutualist sustainable regeneration industry including recycling, transport and energy saving. Mutuals also need better access to 'community venture capital' to start up environmental enterprises. If the framework is right, the environmental economy could become the seed-bed of a new mutual sector in the next century.

4. The future for mutuals

Britain's mutual sector is far larger, more diverse and in better health than is widely thought. Even excluding churches, clubs, voluntary organisations and large membership charities such as the National Trust, which between them have millions of members, the mutual sector provides a significant share of the services we most rely upon: childcare, insurance, health care, education, food and community safety, among others.

Mutual organisations operate in mature industries, such as agri-culture, as well as in the most modern, such as software and elec-tronic commerce. They range from very large organisations, such as Standard Life, the mutual insurer with assets of £50 billion and 4 million customers, to the local, such as the Marsh Lane Family Centre in Sefton. Although some of the longest established mutuals have seen their market share decline – building societies, trade unions, the co-operative movement, friendly societies – there is plenty of evidence of renewal among an army of smaller, often community-based organisations that are embracing the mutual form. And indeed, some older established mutuals have become more competitive in recent years: trade unions, for example, have just recorded their first rise in membership for more than two decades. Other mutuals, such as the WEA, have developed a new role in partnership with the public sector. New mutuals are being formed in health care, community safety and economic development, as well as personal finance and e-commerce.

The demand for mutuals is thus far from exhausted. Mutuals will grow in 'gaps' where consumers feel the state or the market lets them down. When mutuals are well run they excel at sharing and combining the know-how of a large, independent membership, whether that is in the Linux software club or in a health self-help group. That is why mutuals are so suited to the spirit of the times, not just politically but culturally as well: mutuals bring together independent consumers and producers in common endeavour. Mutuals co-ordinate the activities of many independent actors, without either the bureaucracy of a large organisation or the atomisation of an open market.

Types of mutual

Mutuals come in many different shapes and sizes. In the course of this research we have identified three dimensions to categorise a mutual.

Ownership and ethos

Mutuals differ in the degree of mutual ownership involved. A formal ownership mutual is owned by its members. The building societies, mutual insurers and trade unions are the largest ownership mutuals. The advantage of mutual ownership is that there are no outside investors to satisfy. However, mutuals based on mutual ownership can be difficult to form because members have to make a financial commitment and their mutual ownership is no guarantee that they will have a mutual ethos.

Most of the organisations profiled in this report are mutual in ethos but not in ownership. They involve members in both day-to-day decisions and democratic governance, but the members do not necessarily own the organisation. A mutual ethos can be developed in organisations where there are no owners (many charities); where ownership is unclear (many universities and clubs); in public sector organisations that are funded by tax payers (nurseries and schools for example) and in joint ventures where the ownership is shared (many public–private partnerships or projects such as the Sheffield Bond). It is virtually impossible for an organisation to develop a mutual ethos if it is investor owned.

The prospects for mutuality, we argue, will turn less on the creation of fully-fledged ownership mutuals and more on existing kinds of organisation acquiring a mutual ethos.

Commercial or social mutuals

Commercial mutuals, such as agricultural co-operatives and employee owned businesses, operate in markets where they compete with investor owned companies, producing products and services. Social mutuals generally have a social purpose and output in areas such as health, education, community development and crime prevention.

In both commercial and social mutuals, mutuality plays a dual role. The involvement of members helps to determine the organisation's overall purpose and also the way it goes about its business – its internal processes. Community mutuals, such as development trusts, involve people in deciding what direction a community should take. As a result, they also organise their work in a different way, involving more direct community involvement. All successful mutuals adopt this twin-track approach: they combine mutuality in purpose and in process.

Although some commercial mutuals – building societies, mutual insurers and the co-operative retailers – have seen their market share decline, commercial mutuals should be strengthened by several developments. Co-operatives may form in industries that face radical restructuring and price competition, such as reinsurance. Employee owned businesses should become more common as a business model favoured in fast growth, knowledge-intensive industries. Electronic mutuals, such as the Linux club and local electronic auction markets, are likely to become more common. Consumer mutuals might be created, for example, to band together consumers to jointly purchase energy at a discount in liberalised utility markets.

The most exciting prospects are for mutuals that combine commercial and social purposes, for example community credit unions aim to make enough of a financial return to be self-sustaining. Community mutuals, which complement, deliver or compete with public services, could also play a much larger role in future, particularly if the state embarks on a 'mutualisation' programme in the public sector.

Reactive and innovative mutuals

A reactive mutual is created in response to a clear failure by the state or the market, which leaves a group (usually consumers) worse off. The pre-school groups, for example, were formed in response to the lack of adequate state or private nursery provision. Contact a Family was created because parents were dissatisfied with the treatment their children were getting from public services. The mutual insurance industry was created because initially consumers felt they could not trust shareholder owned companies.

Innovative mutuals, on the other hand, are formed to bring together independent people (usually producers) in a joint project to share their know-how. The classic modern example of this is the Linux project, which brought together a group of enthusiasts with similar expertise and interests. Other types of innovative mutuals, such as Communities That Care and self-help mutuals in education and health, are designed to generate ideas by combining people with diverse kinds of know-how. A reactive mutual is set up to solve a particular problem facing a clear constituency; an innovative mutual is set up with a more open-ended goal to tap and share the know-how of like-minded people. In practice of course, the line between the two types is often blurred.

Mutuals will not prosper simply because the political climate becomes more conducive. They will only thrive if they provide an effective organisational response to people's needs. Mutuals have to deliver and be innovative to survive. Our research has identified a set of features which characterise successful mutuals.

Conditions for success

A mutual can succeed only with a clear focus to hold together its members. That focus might be a common need that the mutual can serve, such as demand for affordable insurance or the marketing of agricultural products. Another focus is a sense of community, a shared specialist project or a shared occupation or employer.

As its membership becomes larger and more diverse, it is more difficult for a mutual to succeed because it is harder to forge a decisive common bond. As a result, the sense of membership can be diluted to the point where it becomes meaningless. This is why there have never been 'mutual conglomerates' serving a wide variety of markets. A mutual thrives with a clear focus that holds together its members without requiring a constant re-negotiation of their sense of purpose.

The only slight exception to this rule is a thriving community mutual. A community mutual, with a strong sense of locality, can help people access a wide range of services. This is how the Marsh Lane

Family Centre succeeded by offering parents more than just a nursery. Marsh Lane's success depended on it having a clear purpose (helping families in need) not simply delivering a product (a nursery). However, even successful community mutuals need a clear pitch to attract and retain members. The Speke Community Credit Union, for example, stresses that its capacity to deliver competitive financial services is the basis for its role as a focus for community development. It is this combination that matters: delivering a competitive, first-class service within a community setting. The two must go together.

A successful mutual delivers a tangible sense of membership that is reinforced by members' regular transactions with the organisation. Farmers are members of marketing and supply co-operatives not primarily because they believe in the ethic of co-operation, but because they know it delivers real benefits. The value of membership has to be evident in the quality of service that members get. This every-day reminder of the rewards of membership is far more important than the largely symbolic democratic rights to involvement that members have through the annual general meeting.

The best mutuals spread a culture of membership; it is not written into their constitution. The Leeds City Credit Union and the Oxford, Swindon and Gloucester Co-operative have both shown how mutuals can train staff to communicate the value of membership by involving members more in decisions that directly affect the service they get.

Mutuals have a proven capacity for involving people who are often beyond the reach of the state or the private sector. The most impressive community credit unions, for example, deal with people who the large clearing banks would regard as too much of a risk. The WEA and other lifelong learning organisations reach students who are often ill at ease with formal institutions of learning. Mutuals can get closer to their customers and members than large, formal organisations.

That capacity to reach and involve people who might feel ill at ease with larger organisations is partly due to the kind of know-how mutuals command. Mike Knight, who runs the Speke Community Credit Union, and Sandi Alexander, who runs the Marsh Lane Family Centre, both have a large stock of tacit know-how built up over many years in their communities, which allows them to understand and deal with their members more effectively than organisations that are more detached. Access to local tacit knowledge is just one component of the knowledge-creating potential of mutuals.

Mutuals often combine the formal knowledge of outside experts with the informal know-how of members. This is why the health groups set up by Contact a Family are so potent. They combine the know-how that parents have built up by caring for children with rare medical conditions with the formal know-how of health professionals. The Communities That Care programme, and many other community development initiatives, are designed to combine local expertise with that of outside professionals.

Mutuals can also have distinct advantages in innovation and knowledge creation by drawing on their members' ideas. That capacity to draw in ideas from many different sources is one reason why networked forms of organisation are increasingly common in knowledge-intensive sectors of the economy, such as biotechnology.

Community mutuals in particular provide people with a clear sense of 'ownership' often lacking in public and private community development programmes. People are likely to feel more goodwill and trust to community mutuals than towards the public or private sector.

Downsides to mutuals

Established mutuals can become closed, inward looking and conservative. Just as an investor owned company can become too dominated by the needs of shareholders, a mutual can become too focused only on its existing, core membership. As a result, mutuals can fail to innovate and draw in new members.

Although the membership structure of mutuals means they do not have to face the pressure of delivering returns to shareholders, this can become a weakness if managers are allowed too cosy a life and take their members for granted. Shareholder owned companies can put managers under too much short-term pressure to deliver; but mutuals can put managers under too little pressure.

Some mutuals that are answerable to a strong, local, membership network find it difficult to take on a more ambitious, national tasks. Community mutuals may require a stronger national or regional management capacity, as well as external auditing, to play a larger role in public programmes.

These weaknesses matter most when mutuals face structural shifts in their markets that demand them to come up with a radically innovative response. A mutual that has become too concerned with its current members and that lacks a capacity for strategic thinking may fail to recognise and meet these challenges. Mutuals may take longer to respond to radical changes in the competitive environment than investor owned companies (although many investor owned companies find the task difficult).

Finally, mutuals also have a problem at the start-up stage, as the experience of community credit unions shows. Mutuals thrive on member involvement: that is why it is so difficult to get them started through an act of policy. Yet it is very difficult to get a mutual started, offering a high quality of service, if it is staffed only by volunteers. A mutual, like most organisations, needs a core of professional, full-time managers. In addition, regulatory requirements mean that it is difficult to create mutuals in some areas. Only one building society has been formed in the past few years.

In sum, mutuals succeed when they dynamically combine their different strengths, bringing together local know-how and commitment with professional expertise and management in an organisation that delivers a tangible and valuable sense of membership. When a mutual develops this culture it can set up a potent cycle of trust, commitment and innovation.

Mutuals need an open, transparent, information-rich culture, in which members feel a clear sense of common purpose. The quality of management is critical. Managing a mutual well means orchestrating a process of dynamic combination: to use the distinctive strengths of a mutual to deliver a first class product. This report has provided a string of case studies – Leeds City, Speke Community Credit Union, the WEA, CMG – where managers have done just that.

The environment for mutuals

State regulation plays a critical role shaping the environment in which mutuals compete. The conversion movement among building societies, for example, started in the context of the wider deregulation of the financial services industry. Both the growth and decline of trade unions was in part influenced by legislation governing their activities.

The co-operative retailing movement's decline gathered pace, according to many observers, with the abolition of retail price maintenance, which undermined its famous 'dividend' scheme. Friendly societies contracted sharply only after the Second World War when the welfare state took over many of their functions. Pre-school groups blame their recent closures on the growth of state nursery provision and the introduction of the minimum wage, which has increased their costs. The public sector is often the main competitor to mutuals – especially in health, education and welfare services. In commercial sectors – financial services and retailing, for example – the state plays a critical role as the regulator, which determines whether mutuals are at a competitive disadvantage with other kinds of organisation.

Enlightened state regulation should aim to promote an ecology of competing types of organisation that is diverse enough to promote innovation and pressure for continuous improvements in performance. Requisite variety of organisational forms should become a new goal for competition policy. However, there also limits to how far state initiative can go: the case of the community credit unions highlights the pitfalls of trying to create mutuals as an act of policy without a deep enough grounding in the community.

What is the state's proper role in creating a regulatory framework that treats mutuals fairly? The most pressing issue is to clear up the law governing the ownership of mutuals. Should the members of a mutual have the right to wind it up and if so should they be able to benefit from the proceeds?

In Germany and France there are restrictions on the winding-up of a mutual that have prevented carpet-bagging of the kind seen recently in the UK. These restrictions are one reason why mutual banks account for 37 per cent of retail deposits in France, 35 per cent in the Netherlands and about 30 per cent in Germany. Co-operative banks have 19.3 per cent of all deposits in Germany. In many continental European countries the owners of mutual banks are prevented from taking any benefit from selling their shares in the event of a conversion. Would such restrictions be justified in the UK? Members should have a right to wind-up a mutual, otherwise its claims to be a democratic members' organisation would be hollow. A failing mutual, a building society going bankrupt or a cricket club that could not raise a team, should be wound up. However, winding up a clear failure is quite different from turning a healthy and competitive mutual into an investor owned organisation to satisfy the short-term financial interest of members and executives who want to earn a windfall.

In practice, distinguishing between these motives for winding up might be difficult. An alternative test would distinguish between different classes of membership. It should be possible for mutuals to admit into full voting membership only members who pledge to abide by mutual principles and to keep the organisation mutual. This would not preclude other categories of non-voting membership, and the mutual could continue to serve non-members. Such a law would mean that a mutual could be wound up only when it had genuinely failed to serve its purpose, rather than to satisfy the financial interests of current members.

One model for such a restriction is the rule introduced by the Nationwide Building Society, which has said that new members would have to donate the proceeds of a conversion to a charity. That has reduced the incentive for carpet-baggers to join the society and helped to ensure that the membership is less likely to be swayed by short-term financial gains. The case for such a restricted membership is twofold. First, the current members might be the custodians of the mutual but they are not necessarily its full owners, anymore than we are the owners of our genes which have been passed down to us through years of evolution. Even strong mutuals such as the Nationwide are the product of a shared, fuzzy ownership. Second, such a restriction would preserve a greater diversity of organisational forms in the economy and so would have wider benefits in terms of competition and choice.

The case against such a restriction is simple: mutuals with relatively closed membership lists focus on satisfying those members with a vote. They can become conservative and slow-moving. Mutuals face unsettling conversion votes, but quoted companies face take-over threats that can be equally destabilising.

These issues are finely balanced. To nurture the nascent mutuals and preserve what remains of the established mutual movement, the government should extend the scope of its review of company law to include a re-assessment of the laws governing the ownership of mutuals. An alternative would be to create a Royal Commission on Ownership to examine the case for stronger protections for mutual forms of ownership in the new economy. For example, community credit unions cannot be wound up to profit their members in the way that building societies can. Without new legislation to protect mutuality there is a danger that the menu of organisational choices open to us will get shorter and poorer, leaving us a choice between the state, the private sector and various forms of joint venture between the two.

The laws of ownership governing mutuals are just one area where the state will play a critical role. Another will be the promotion of mutuality through the Best Value programme governing contracting out among local authorities. Community mutuals such as pre-school groups can deliver significant 'unaudited' benefits, which might not be taken into account by councils examining how to reorganise services to deliver best value. To give mutuals a chance to compete with public sector providers, the government needs to make sure that rules governing contracting out take into account the role of mutuals. A test case of the government's ability to promote a dynamic ecology of different kinds of organisations will be nursery provision, where some of the expansion of state provision is at the expense of long-established mutuals. An enlightened policy would involve market regulation to ensure that parents have choice between different kinds of nursery provision, not just the lowest cost, mass provision.

The state can play a huge role in promoting mutuality, in delivering and reorganising public services, but it needs to recognise the value of promoting a mixed economy of different and competing organisations – mutual, state, private, charitable and hyrbids of all four – within a sector. That means framing policy not just to deliver value for money in the short-run but to encourage the requisite diversity of organisations within a sector to keep it competitive. This goal of requisite variety could become in time an explicit goal of competition policy.

Alongside state regulation to promote a diversity of organisations to deliver public policy, the mutuals need to improve their managerial capacity. In common with other organisations, public and private, mutuals have faced large structural shifts in markets, competition, culture and technology. Building societies have faced competition from banks; the co-operative retailers have faced the rise of Tesco and out-of-town superstores; the labour market has shifted and shaken beneath the trade unions. These structural shifts have tested the ability of established mutuals to respond. Mutuals have been too slow to innovate products, services and organisational structures. They will only play a larger role in delivering publicly funded programmes, for example in health and education, if they show how a loose, federated movement of organisations that prize their local independence can be brought together to meet national targets and standards. Other mutuals need to follow the example of the WEA, which has combined local independence with national strategy.

The new mutuals, such as community foundations, development trusts and community credit unions, which are often locally based, need stronger regional and national bodies that can promote best practice, share economies of scale and help set the strategic direction for the movement as a whole. The credit union movement needs more local bodies such as the Birmingham Credit Union Development Agency as well as a single national organisation that can provide support services for community credit unions, along the lines of the national service centre for credit unions in Australia.

Proposals for mutual development

1. A 'mutualisation' programme for the public sector

Our most radical and far-reaching proposal is that the government should launch a 'mutualisation' programme in the public sector. This would be a successor to the privatisation programme of the 1980s. People are generally suspicious of privatisation reaching deep into the heart of public services such as health and education; yet they also acknowledge the shortcomings of the overly bureaucratic and inflexible forms of state provision. A 'mutualisation' programme could reach into social and public housing, public health, childcare and nursery education, crime prevention, adult education, lifelong learning, community regeneration, recycling and many other sectors. In these areas people want services that are not-for-profit and inclusive and that are also responsive to local and special needs.

A 'mutualisation' programme would provide the government with a way to reduce the size of the public sector without either reducing social provision or eroding the civic ethos of public services. Indeed, a mutualisation programme would probably strengthen the civic culture by decentralising state provision without bringing in the private sector and the market. In its small way the Marsh Lane Family Centre, which became a model for all the nurseries within Sefton, is an example of the potential of this mutualisation programme to reconstitute the public sector along mutual lines. A mutualistation programme would be more difficult to implement than the privatisation programme, which transferred assets from one form of ownershp to another with the help of City advisers. A mutualisation programme would involve creating new organisational forms and involving a much wider group of users and partners. It would need to proceed through several stages, including, firstly, the government encouraging local authorities to work more imaginatively with local mutuals.

2. Mutual–public partnerships
A precusor to fully-fledged mutualisation of the state would be to develop 'mutual–public partnerships' in which mutuals would become the preferred delivery vehicle for a range of government programmes, especially those focused on community and neighbourhood renewal, crime prevention, community safety, public health and childcare. A working example of such a mutual–public partnership is the relationship between the Workers' Education Association and its public sector partners such as the Further Education Funding Council and local authorities. These partnerships combine the local know-how and commitment of mutuals with the resources and strategic capacity of the public sector.

Crime prevention is an excellent candidate for such a strategy. The police alone cannot deliver community safety and must rely heavily on community trust and knowledge. A way to harness this could be the development of crime prevention mutuals, formalising the kind of police–community partnership that is emerging in areas such as Balsall Heath and paying them for crime prevention services such as local crime audits, for delivery of preventive schemes such as Youth Works and for Street Watch programmes. Such mutuals could also become employers of concierges and community safety officers in tower blocks and social housing estates, working in partnership with tenants' associations.

3. Mutuals complementing the public sector

Mutuals could play a growing role in complementing state provision by providing services that the public sector finds difficult to deliver. We increasingly live in a mixed economy of welfare in which people are more likely to move between public and private providers of health, education and other services, using the public sector for some services but turning to the private sector for others. Mutuals could play a leading role in this new mixed economy. One example is the role of the Benenden Health Society, which focuses on providing its members with services that the NHS can only deliver after a long wait. Another is the Unison plan for a top-up stakeholder pension for people on low incomes who will not have a sufficient state pension but cannot afford a fully private pension.

4. Community development

Mutuals are gathering a critical mass in community development, with community foundations, community loan funds, development trusts, city bond schemes, Local Exchange and Trading Schemes and community credit unions. The potential for this community finance sector is shown by the scale of community foundations and credit unions in the United States. Britain should aim to create a similarly robust community finance and reinvestment sector in the next ten years, for example, by aiming to create a 'local bond' investment scheme or community foundation in every city with more than 100,000 people. Proctor and Gamble have led the way in the private sector by donating £1 million to fund a community foundation scheme. A radical proposal would be to require large companies that declare large-scale redundancies to invest in a community foundation in the wake of a factory or plant closure. This is an area where central and local government, the private sector and local groups need to combine to develop a concerted community-focused approach.

One way to do this could be to take up the community worker Bob Holman's proposal for the creation of a National Neighbourhood Fund, allowing small community groups – many of them nascent mutuals – to bid for funds to build up skills and develop local projects.[47]

5. Mutual partnerships and mergers

One route for established mutuals to renew themselves is to ally with younger mutuals. Mergers and joint ventures between mutuals should become more common. An example is the way Unison has co-operated with financial services mutuals to develop a pension plan for low-income savers. Another is the role that Leeds City Credit Union is playing in fostering smaller credit unions in its area. Mutuals have often failed to capitalise on their strengths. Many would benefit from creating umbrella organisations to spread good practice and to offer support services to one another. One possibility would be for mutuals to band together to sponsor an MBA programme or learning network tailored to the needs of managers in mutual businesses, or to set up a Mutual Business School (which could be a virtual network available over the Internet or BBC) offering a wide variety of courses in management and in the art of community partnerships and community development.

6. Mutual–private joint ventures

Another possibility would be for mutuals to form joint ventures with large private sector companies to combine their distinctive strengths. This is one possible way for credit unions to develop, for instance through the model of co-operation that NatWest Bank is exploring with the Birmingham Credit Union Development Agency. Credit unions could provide the banks with a gateway to less affluent customers, who the banks cannot afford or do not know how to reach. The banks would provide the local credit unions with back office services and channel products to them – insurance and mortgages, for example – that credit unions cannot yet provide.

7. Electronic mutuals

Among the most promising avenues for mutuals to grow and emerge are the Internet and electronic networks. Linux is one of the most innovative business organisations to emerge for decades: it is founded on co-operative self-help. This mutual approach to consumption and production is ideally suited to the Internet and the 'communities' of consumption and practice it is creating.

8. Employee ownership

Employee ownership is a form of mutuality which should flower in the knowledge-driven economy as a way of allowing key knowledge workers in particular to share in the wealth they are creating. In the US, especially in new software and media businesses, young knowledge-workers expect to be paid in part in equity and stock options. This culture should be encouraged in the UK.

9. Consumer mutuals for energy

The liberalisation of markets for the supply of gas and electricity creates considerable opportunities for consumer mutuals to bring people together to benefit from bulk purchasing schemes. Liberalised, more competitive markets for gas and electricity disproportionately benefit better-off, more sophisticated consumers. Poorer consumers often rely on pre-paid meters for gas and electricity. Some relatively poor rural areas are not connected to the gas network. One possibility would be for gas consumers in an area to band together to jointly purchase gas and electricity in the bulk market, along the lines of schemes pioneered by Neighbourhood Energy Action. Joint-purchasing could allow less affluent consumers to band together to reap the benefits of liberalisation. Such a fuel co-operative is being run by non-profit Equigas, which is working in partnership with Southern Electricity. A different approach, applicable to rural areas and housing estates, would be for mutuals to exploit advances in technology that will allow local areas to use small gas-powered generators to make their own electricity.

10. Mutual housing

The opportunities for promoting mutual housing are largely unexplored in the UK. In contrast, in the US the condominium is the fastest growing form of housing. Non-state social housing schemes are much more common in parts of continental Europe. Progress in this area will turn on whether the government legislates to introduce a form of commonhold ownership.

These are some of the most promising avenues along which mutuals could develop. It is a far from exhaustive list. The National Lottery could be turned into a mutual the next time the franchise comes up for auction. The BBC could become one of the largest electronic and educational mutuals, using its brand and reputation to create an electronic university or learning club. Waste recycling and community environment projects lend themselves to mutual approaches in which people share responsibility for upgrading their environment. In an economy where most of employment and output will come from small businesses, the mutual guarantee societies common in Continental Europe may come into their own. Mutuals can and must recapture their reputation for innovation and dynamism. Much of that depends on the quality of their managers and the incentives and pressures they are under to react entrepreneurially to change.

Mutuality is far from dead and buried. Quite the opposite: mutual, networked organisations, which stand between the public and the private sectors, the state and the community, could be among the most dynamic in the new economy. The Blair government could make a lasting mark on the pattern of ownership and social provision in Britain by embarking on a mutualisation programme that could be as radical in the long run as the Conservatives' privatisations proved to be. Mutuality was a big idea in the last century: it can be again in the next. Mutuality is not finished – unleashing its potential should be one of the priorities of New Labour's second term.

Notes

1. Hargreaves I, 1999, *In From the Cold: Co-operatives and social exclusion*, UK Co-operative Council, Manchester.
2. Etzioni A, 1993, *The Spirit of Community*, Crown, New York; Mulgan G, 1997, *Connexity*, Chatto & Windus, London.
3. Kay J, 1993, *The Foundations of Corporate Success*, Oxford University Press, Oxford; Hutton W, 1995, *The State We're In*, Cape, London; Kochan TS and Osterman P, 1994, *The Mutual Gains Enterprise*, Harvard Business School Press, Boston, Massachusetts. Other books with a similar theme include: de Gues A, 1997, *The Living Company*, Harvard Business School Press, Boston, Massachusetts; Wheeler D and Sillanpaa M, 1997, *The Stakeholder Corporation*, Pitman, London; Riechheld F, 1996, *The Loyalty Effect*, Harvard Business School Press, Boston, Massachusetts.
4. Ridley M, 1996, *The Origins of Virtue*, Viking, London.
5. Kraemer S and Roberts J, eds, 1996, *The Politics of Attachment*, Free Association Books, London.
6. Moore J, 1996, *The Death of Competition*, John Wiley, Chichester; Nalebuff B and Brandenburger A, 1996, *Co-opetition*, HarperCollinsBusiness, London.
7. Giddens A, 1998, *The Third Way: The Renewal of Social Democracy*, Polity Press, Cambridge.
8. This history is set out in Henry Hansmann's *The Ownership of Enterprise* (1996, Belknap Press, Cambridge, Massachusetts).
9. Alexander T, 1997, *Family Learning*, Demos, London.
10. TUC, 1998, *Union Gateways to Learning*, TUC, London.
11. See Clough B, 1997, 'Union Partnerships for Lifelong Learning', *Local Economy*, November.
12. Bentley T, *New Statesman*, 'Mutuality: The caring, sharing society', special supplement, 19 March 1999.
13. See Leadbeater C, 1997, *The Rise of the Social Entrepreneur*, Demos, London, for a case study of the Eldonians housing scheme in Liverpool as an example.
14. UK Co-operative Council, 1998, *Co-operative Housing*, UKCC, Manchester.
15. Community Self-Build Agency, 1998, Information Sheet A5, CSBA, London.
16. Price Waterhouse, 1995, *Tenants in Control*, HMSO, London.
17. Walter Segal Self-Build Trust, *You Build* magazine, issue 17, August 1998.
18. See for example Taylor M, 1995, *Unleashing the Potential: Bringing residents to the centre of regeneration*, Joseph Rowntree Foundation, York; Carley M and Kirk K, 1998, *Sustainable by 2020? A strategic approach to urban regeneration for Britain's cities*, Policy Press, Bristol.
19. See Leadbeater, 1997 (note 13).
20. For more details on these and other examples of innovation in housing policy see Greenhalgh L, 1998, *Habitat: reconnecting housing to city policy*, Comedia, Stroud.
21. UK Co-operative Council, 1998 (note 14).
22. Young M and Lemos G, 1997, *The Communities We Have Lost and Can Regain*, Lemos and Crane, London.
23. For more details of the South Shore record see Leadbeater C, 1999 [forthcoming] *Living on Thin Air: The new economy*, Viking, London.
24. See Bright J, 1997, *Turning the Tide: Crime, community and prevention*, Demos, London.
25. NACRO, 1999, *Reducing Conflict, Building communities*, NACRO, London.
26. See Bright, 1997 (note 24).
27. Atkinson D, 1997, *Reclaiming the Streets*,

Phoenix Centre, Birmingham.
28. Bentley T and Gurumurthy R, 1999, *Destination Unknown: Engaging with the problems of marginalised youth*, Demos, London.
29. See Bright, 1997 (note 24).
30. Youth Action [undated], *Partners for Life: Young people and community safety*, Crime Concern/Prudential, London.
31. Pollard S et al, 1994, *Towards a More Co-operative Society*, Independent Healthcare Association, London.
32. Wilkinson D and Applebee E, 1999, *Implementing Holistic Government*, Policy Press, Bristol.
33. ICOM, 1998, *Co-operating in Care*, UKCC, Manchester.
34. Gaskin K and Vincent J, 1996, *Co-operating for Health*, CRSP, Loughborough University, Loughborough.
35. Lloyd D, 1999, 'Sustainability, Health and the Environment', *Environment and Health*, issue 6.
36. Hallows N, 1998, 'Future Health', *BMA News Review*, 16 May.
37. See case study in Leadbeater C and Goss S, 1998, *Civic Entrepreneurship*, Demos, London.
38. John Moores University report on credit unions.
39. Leadbeater C, 1998, *The Employee Mutual*, Demos, London.
40. Hagel J and Armstrong AG, 1997, *Net Gain: Expanding markets through virtual communities*, Harvard Business School Press, Boston, Massachusetts.
41. Malon TW and Laubacher RJ, 1998, 'The dawn of the e-lance economy', *Harvard Business Review*, vol 76, no 5.
42. This is a classic strategy for innovating firms in new technology industries. See *The Innovators Dilemma* (Christiansen C, 1997, Harvard Business School Press, Boston, Massachusetts).
43. Rowan W, 1997, *Guaranteed Electronic Markets: The backbone of a twenty-first century economy?*, Demos, London.
44. See Worpole K, 1997, 'A green space beyond self-interest', *New Statesman*, 30 May.
45. Murray R and Collins K, 1998, *Reinventing Waste*, Ecologika, London; Murray R, 1999 [forthcoming], *Working Cities: Wealth and jobs in the recycling sector*, Demos, London.
46. Fagan G, 1998, 'Education and engagement for sustainability: the CADISPA approach' in Warburton D, ed, *Community and Sustainable Development*, Earthscan, London.
47. Holman B, 'A modest proposal against inequality', in *The Good Life*, Demos Collection issue 14, 1998; Holman B, 1998, *Faith in the Poor*, Lion.